CW00486008

TUNE IN FOR FEAR

With the same editor:

Hallow'een Hauntings
Ghost Tour
Nightcaps and Nightmares
Greasepaint and Ghosts
Christmas Spirits
Dead of Night

TUNE IN
FOR FEAR

A Choice of Supernatural
Radio Stories

Edited by
Peter Haining

WILLIAM KIMBER · LONDON

This collection first published in 1985 by
WILLIAM KIMBER & CO. LIMITED
100 Jermyn Street, London SW1Y 6EE

The collection © Peter Haining 1985
© Estate of H.G. Wells 1920
© Estate of Eden Phillpotts 1936
© Estate of A.J. Alan 1928
© Estate of Marjorie Bowen 1935
© Nelson Bond 1937
© Estate of Alonzo Deen Cole 1936
© Robert Bloch 1944
© Ray Bradbury 1951
© John Dickson Carr 1945
© Estate of Algernon Blackwood 1906

ISBN 0 7183 0558 2

*This book is copyright. No part of it may be reproduced
in any form without permission in writing from the
publishers except by a reviewer who wishes to quote
brief passages in a review written for inclusion in a
newspaper, magazine, radio or television broadcast.*

Photoset in North Wales by
Derek Doyle & Associates Mold, Clwyd
and printed in Great Britain by
Biddles Limited, Guildford, Surrey

Contents

For
Frank and Linda Peacock
Good friends …
and Good Listeners.

Acknowledgements

The Editor is grateful to the following authors, their agents or executors for permission to use copyright material in this collection: Messrs. A.P. Watt for 'The Invasion From Mars' by H.G. Wells and 'A Haunted Island' by Algernon Blackwood; Hutchinson & Co Ltd for 'Terror From The Sea' by Eden Phillpotts and 'The Diver' by A.J. Alan; The Executors of Marjorie Bowen for 'Incubus'; Charles Scribner & Sons for 'Mr Mergenthwirker's Lobblies' by Nelson Bond; The Executors of Alonzo Deen Cole for 'Mrs Hawker's Will; A.M. Heath Ltd for 'The Bat Is My Brother' by Robert Bloch; A.D. Peters Ltd for 'The Screaming Woman' by Ray Bradbury; The Executors of John Dickson Carr for 'The Other Hangman'.

Introduction

'I like radio better than television
because I can see the pictures better.'

At first this quotation may seem like a contradiction in terms. How can you possibly *see* something better that you can only *hear*? Yet, if we stop and think for a moment, there is a simple and very compelling logic about it. For in watching television, the pictures are those that the director has devised for us to see. But when we listen to the radio the pictures in our minds are our *own*. And they can be so much more effective!

The quote was actually made by a small boy in 1974 when he was approached by a representative of *Reader's Digest* conducting a survey into whether people preferred radio or television. His answer crystallised an attitude that is not only quite widespread, but perhaps more specifically underlines a feeling that radio is much the better medium for tales of imagination – the supernatural in particular. For as the scholar Julia Briggs wrote a few years later in 1977: 'Sound broadcasting is a particularly good medium for ghost stories as it has strong powers of suggestion (creaking doors, weird cries) yet none of that over-explicit realisation that often undermines the horrific when presented visually, on television or in films.'

This is a view I happen to share myself. And I can tell you how it came to be formed from an experience way back in my childhood in the 1940's. In those days of the infancy of television, I used to get great pleasure from listening to the radio for an hour or so before I went to sleep. Quite often, there was a creepy play or story that would take my interest.

One night, after just such a programme, my mother found me hiding, shivering, under the bedclothes. Naturally, she asked what was wrong.

'It was the radio story,' I whispered. 'It was so frightening I turned it off.'

'What?' she exclaimed. 'After all those things you stare at on television and in films?'

'Oh, yes,' I replied, blinking furiously from under the sheets. 'On television I can *see* it – that's not half so scary!'

I sometimes think it is difficult for young people today to realise just what a hold the radio had on the public imagination in those twenty years from 1930 to 1950 which have been described as the 'Golden Age' of broadcasting. The development of the transmission and reception of radio waves by Marconi at the turn of the century and then the intervention of the radio valve in 1904 had paved the way for public broadcasting in 1920. And then with the introduction of the wireless set into homes all over Britain, America and even further afield, a whole new world of experience was opened up to listeners wherever they might be. The latest news from the far corners of the earth, developments and discoveries in science and technology, quiz shows, talks, dramas, discussion programmes – all were available at the turn of a switch.

Sometimes the impact of radio on people was greater than anyone had imagined. It could instruct and educate them, certainly. But it could also mystify and even frighten them, albeit not intentionally. Nowhere was this more evident than when producers and actors brought tales of the supernatural to their listening audiences. Through their skills they could make people *believe* in the invisible, the monstrous and the terrifying. From the 1920's for almost half a century such programmes reigned supreme; and even when radio lost its position of pre-eminence as in-home entertainment to the 'box', the power of the air waves somehow to give a weird tale the edge in a listener's mind rather than in his eyes remained undiminished.

And that, in a nutshell, is what this collection has been brought together to commemorate. As a reminder of some of the great programmes and great stories that week-by-week made listeners on either side of the Atlantic 'tune in for fear'.

Himan Brown, one of the American pioneers of radio mystery shows – a man who is still active as a producer today – has nicely summarised why this appeal has proved so enduring. 'I think "listening" is terribly important,' he said in an interview a short while ago. 'We are giving people the opportunity, the thrill, of using their imaginations through radio drama. It's the most personal form of theatre I know.

'There are those who say that TV is everything. But I think radio is just as potent and meaningful a form of entertainment. And suffice it to say that all the actors who work for me are from the theatre and motion pictures and they are delighted to do radio dramas because it is such an uninhibited medium of expression. No make-up, no costumes, no worrying about the learning of lines and all that. I feel that radio drama is a form of theatre: it isn't a stunt, it isn't nostalgia. It's the theatre of the mind – a vital, meaningful world of entertainment.'

The vitality of the medium has, in truth, been underlined of late by the fact that apart from the dedicated attention of those who were around during the Golden Age, a younger generation so used to having everything served up in pictures, is also discovering the joys of listening and *imagining* things which are offered by the radio.

Tune In For Fear is for both of these groups. A nostalgic trip into memory for older fans of *Mercury Theatre, Nightmares, Inner Sanctum* and *Appointment With Fear* as well as a look at radio's more recent successes such as *Mystery Theatre* and *Spinechillers*. Along the way, too, we shall be meeting those unforgettable hosts whose graveyard tones took us each week into strange and frightening worlds – men like A.J.Alan, Raymond Johnson and my own favourite, the sinister 'Man in Black'.

There are still many people who believe that radio can provide more genuine thrills for the imagination than either television or films: and in this book I think you will find some of the best stories that have helped them do just that. Certainly, they represent the power of the tale of mystery and imagination at its most potent.

In conclusion, I doubt very much that we shall ever again have quite such a panic as Orson Welles' radio version of 'The War of the Worlds' created in 1938 when literally thousands of terrified listeners took to their cars to escape what they were convinced was a genuine invasion from Space. But if we *are* prepared to allow our minds free rein under the seductive power of the radio and the kind of superb stories to be found in the pages which follow, who can be *quite* sure ...

Peter Haining
August,1984.

I

The Invasion from Mars

H.G.Wells

The most famous supernatural radio broadcast of all is, without question, Orson Welles' adaptation of his namesake H.G.Wells' classic story 'The War of the Worlds' which went out over the air waves of America on the very appropriate night of Hallowe'en in 1938 and so convinced many listeners that an actual Martian invasion was taking place that they fled in panic from their homes all across the country. This broadcast is still a legend in America and is invariably quoted whenever the suitability or otherwise of any similar kind of programme – be it on radio or television – is brought into question. The rest of the world is also familiar with the forty-five minute show produced by Orson Welles for CBS's weekly Sunday evening programme, Mercury Theatre, *for it generated newspaper headlines everywhere: some as startling as the* New York Daily News *which screamed in three-inch-high type: FAKE WAR ON RADIO SPREADS PANIC OVER U.S. Orson Welles (then just 23!) claimed that the 'authentic' way in which he presented the drama – by way of increasingly hysterical reports from radio commentators – was intended to be nothing other than a Hallowe'en prank. But this proved a masterly understatement as thousands of people jammed the telephone wires and highways in terror as they tried to escape from what they thought were advancing Martian war machines bent on death and destruction. This extraordinary phenomenon may seem incredible today: but it does clearly illustrate the extraordinary power radio was enjoying during the early years of its Golden Age. Even more extraordinary is the fact that Herbert George Wells (1866-1946), one of the great pioneers of Science Fiction, had actually written his novel some forty years earlier in 1898! In 1920 he also produced a specially condensed version of the story for the* Strand *magazine which highlights all the special*

*elements that Orson Welles utilised to such stunning effect on the radio.
As Welles commented some years later, 'The frightened folks who took to
the hills to get away from the Martians have long since gotten over that
interplanetary hoax' – but any of them re-reading this following version
may well find some frightening memories stirring once again. And even
those who never heard 'The Panic Broadcast' – as it has become known
in radio history – should have no difficulty in imagining the kind of
scenes that were being created in the minds of listeners gathered
breathlessly around their radio sets almost half a century ago …*

I

A FALLING STAR

The first star was seen early in the morning rushing over
Winchester eastward, high in the atmosphere. Hundreds must
have seen it, and taken it for an ordinary falling star. For in
those days no one gave a thought to the outer worlds of space
as sources of human danger. At most, terrestrial men fancied
there might be other men upon Mars, perhaps inferior to
themselves and ready to welcome a missionary enterprise. Yet
across the gulf of space, minds that are to our minds as ours
are to the beasts that perish, intellects vast and cool and
unsympathetic, regarded this earth with envious eyes, and
slowly and surely drew their plans against us.

No one seems to have troubled to look for the fallen thing
that night. But early in the morning it was found, almost
entirely buried in the sand, among the scattered splinters of a
fir-tree on the common between Horsell, Woking, and
Ottershaw. The uncovered part had the appearance of a huge
cylinder, caked over, and its outline softened, by a thick, scaly,
dun-coloured incrustation. It had a diameter of about thirty
yards. A stirring noise within the cylinder was ascribed at first
to the unequal cooling of its surface, for at that time it did not
occur to anyone that it might be hollow.

When, about sunset, I joined the crowd at the edge of the pit
the thing had dug by its impact with the soil, the end of the
cylinder was being screwed out from within. Nearly two feet of
shining screw projected. Somebody blundered against me, and
I narrowly missed being pitched on the top of the screw. As I

turned to avoid the fall the lid of the cylinder fell upon the gravel with a ringing concussion. For a moment the cavity seemed perfectly black, for I had the sunset in my eyes.

I think everyone expected to see a man emerge – possibly something a little unlike us terrestrial men, but in all essentials a man. I know I did. But, looking, I presently saw something stirring within the shadow – greyish, billowy movements, one above another, and then two luminous discs like eyes. Then something resembling a little grey snake, about the thickness of a walking stick coiled up out of the writhing middle, and wriggled in the air towards me, and then another.

A big, greyish, rounded bulk, the size, perhaps, of a bear, was rising slowly and painfully out of the cylinder. As it bulged up and caught the light, it glistened like wet leather. Two large, dark-coloured eyes were regarding me steadfastly. It was rounded, and had, one might say, a face. There was a mouth under the eyes, the lipless brim of which quivered and panted, and dropped saliva. The body heaved and pulsated convulsively. A lank, tentacular appendage gripped the edge of the cylinder, another swayed in the air.

Those who have never seen a living Martian can scarcely imagine the strange horror of their appearance. The peculiar V-shaped mouth with its pointed upper lip, the absence of brow ridges, the absence of a chin beneath the wedge-like lower lip, the incessant quivering of this mouth, the Gorgon groups of tentacles, the tumultuous breathing of the lungs in a strange atmosphere, the evident heaviness and painfulness of movement, due to the greater gravitational energy of the earth – above all, the extraordinary intensity of the immense eyes – culminated in an effect akin to nausea. There was something fungoid in the oily brown skin, something in the clumsy deliberation of their tedious movements unspeakably terrible. Even at this first encounter, this first glimpse, I was overcome with disgust and dread.

Suddenly the monster vanished. It had toppled over the brim of the cylinder, and fallen into the pit with a thud like the fall of a great mass of leather. I heard it give a peculiar thick cry, and forthwith another of these creatures appeared darkly in the deep shadow of the aperture.

At that my rigour of terror passed away. I turned, and,

running madly, made for the first group of trees, perhaps a hundred yards away; but I ran slantingly and stumbling, for I could not avert my face from these things. There, among some young pine trees and furze bushes, I stopped, panting, and waited further developments. Once a leash of thin black whips, like the arms of an octopus, flashed across the sunset, and was immediately withdrawn, and afterwards a thin rod rose up, joint by joint, bearing at its apex a circular disc that spun with a wobbling motion.

Suddenly there was a flash of light, and a quantity of luminous greenish smoke came out of the pit in three distinct puffs, which drove up, one after the other, straight into the still air. At the same time a faint hissing sound became audible. Beyond the pit stood a little wedge of people, a little knot of small vertical black shapes upon the black ground. As the green smoke rose their faces flashed out pallid green, and faded again as it vanished.

Then slowly the hissing passed into humming, into a long, loud droning noise. Slowly a humped shape rose out of the pit, and the ghost of a beam of light seemed to flicker out from it. Forthwith, flashes of actual flame, a bright glare leaping from one to another, sprang from the scattered group of men. It was as if some invisible jet impinged upon them and flashed into white flame. It was as if each man were suddenly and momentarily turned to fire.

Then, by the light of their own destruction, I saw them staggering and falling, and their supporters turning to run.

I stood staring, not as yet realizing that this was death leaping from man to man in that little distant crowd. All I felt was that it was something strange. An almost noiseless and blinding flash of light, and a man fell headlong and lay still, and as the unseen shaft of heat passed over them, pine trees burst into fire, and every dry furze-bush became with one dull thud a mass of flames. It is still a matter of wonder how the Martians are able to slay men so swiftly and so silently. Many think that in some way they are able to generate an intense heat in a chamber of practically absolute non-conductivity. This intense heat they project in a parallel beam against any object they choose by means of a polished parabolic mirror of unknown composition – much as the parabolic mirror of a lighthouse projects a beam of light. But no one has absolutely proved these details. However it was done, it is certain that a beam of heat is the essence of the matter – heat, and invisible, instead of visible, light. Whatever is combustible flashes into flame at its touch, lead runs like water, it softens iron, cracks and melts glass, and when it falls upon water incontinently that explodes into steam.

That night nearly forty people lay under the starlight about the pit, charred and distorted beyond recognition, and all night long the common from Horsell to Maybury was deserted, and brightly ablaze.

II

FIGHTING BEGINS

It was in a storm that I first saw the Martians at large, on the night of the third falling star. How can I describe the thing I saw? A monstrous tripod, higher than many houses, striding over the young pine trees, and smashing them aside in its career; a walking engine of glittering metal, striding now across the heather, articulate ropes of steel dangling from it, and the clattering tumult of its passage mingling with the riot of the thunder. A flash, and it came out vividly, heeling over one way with two feet in the air, to vanish, and reappear almost instantly, as it seemed, with the next flash, a hundred yards nearer. Can you imagine a milking-stool tilted and bowled violently along the ground? That was the impression those instant flashes gave. But instead of a milking-stool, imagine it a great body of machinery on a tripod stand.

Seen nearer, the thing was incredibly strange, for it was no mere insensate machine driving on its way. Machine it was, with a ringing metallic pace, and long flexible glittering tentacles (one of which gripped a young pine tree) swinging and rattling about its strange body. It picked its road as it went striding along, and the brazen hood that surmounted it moved to and fro with the inevitable suggestion of a head looking about it. Behind the main body was a huge thing of white metal like a gigantic fisherman's basket, and puffs of green smoke squirted out from the joints of the limbs as the monster swept by me.

All that night the creatures were busy – communicating, I

suppose, and maturing their plans. It was not until the next morning that our resistance began. The fighting I saw took place at Shepperton Wey, where a crowd of fugitives were waiting their turn to cross the river by the ferry.

Suddenly we saw a rush of smoke far away up the river, a puff of smoke that jerked up into the air, and hung; and forthwith the ground heaved under foot, and a heavy explosion shook the air, smashing two or three windows in the houses near, and leaving us astonished.

Quickly, one after the other, one, two, three, four of the armoured Martians appeared, far away over the little trees, across the flat meadows that stretch towards Chertsey, and striding hurriedly towards the river. Little cowled figures they seemed at first, going with a rolling motion and as fast as flying birds.

Then, advancing obliquely towards us, came a fifth. Their armoured bodies glittered in the sun as they swept swiftly forward upon the guns, growing rapidly larger as they drew nearer. One on the extreme left – the remotest, that is – flourished a huge case high in the air, and the ghostly terrible heat-ray I had already seen on Friday night smote towards Chertsey, and struck the town.

'Get under water!' I shouted, unheeded. And, as the first Martian towered over head scarcely a couple of hundred feet away, I flung myself under the surface.

When I raised my head, it was on the bank, and, in a stride, wading halfway across. The knees of its foremost legs bent at the further bank, and in another moment it had raised itself to its full height again, close to the village of Shepperton. Forthwith the six guns, which, unknown to anyone on the right bank, had been hidden behind the outskirts of that village, fired simultaneously. The sudden near concussions, the last close upon the first, made my heart jump. The monster was already raising the case generating the heat-ray as the first shell burst six yards above the hood.

Simultaneously two other shells burst in the air near the body as the hood twisted round in time to receive, but not in time to dodge, the fourth shell.

The shell burst clean in the face of the thing. The hood bulged, flashed, was whirled off in a dozen tattered fragments of red flesh and glittering metal.

'Hit!' shouted I, with something between a scream and a cheer.

I heard answering shouts from the people in the water about me. I could have leapt out of the water with that momentary exultation.

The decapitated colossus reeled like a drunken giant, but it did not fall over. It recovered its balance by a miracle, and, no longer heeding its steps, and with the camera that fired the heat-ray now rigidly upheld, it reeled swiftly upon Shepperton. The living intelligence, the Martian within the hood, was slain and splashed to the four winds of heaven, and the thing was now but a mere intricate device of metal whirling to destruction. It drove along in a straight line, incapable of guidance. It struck the tower of Shepperton church, smashing it down as the impact of a battering-ram might have done, swerved aside, blundered on, and collapsed with a tremendous impact into the river out of my sight.

A violent explosion shook the air, and a spout of water, steam, mud, and shattered metal shot far up into the sky. As the camera of the heat-ray hit the water, the latter had incontinently flashed into steam. In another moment a huge wave, like a muddy tidal bore, but almost scalding hot, came sweeping round the bend upstream. I saw people struggling shorewards, and heard their screaming faintly above the seething and roar of the Martian's collapse.

Then again I ducked, for the other Martians were advancing. When for a moment I raised my head to take breath and throw the water from my eyes, the steam was rising in a whirling white fog that at first hid the Martians altogether. The noise was deafening. Then I saw them dimly, colossal figures of grey, magnified by the mist. They had passed by me, and two were stooping over the tumultuous ruins of their comrade.

The third and fourth stood beside him in the water, one perhaps two hundred yards from me, the other towards Laleham. The generators of the heat-rays waved high, and the hissing beams smote down this way and that.

The air was full of sound, a deafening and confusing conflict of noises, the clangorous din of the Martians, the crash of falling houses, the thud of trees, fences, sheds, flashing into flame, and the crackling and roaring of fire. Dense black smoke was leaping up to mingle with the steam from the river, and as the heat-ray went to and fro over Weybridge, its impact was marked by flashes of incandescent white, that gave place at once to a smoky dance of lurid flames.

For a moment, perhaps, I stood there, breast-high in the almost boiling water, dumbfounded at my position, hopeless of escape. Through the reek I could see the people who had been with me in the river scrambling out of the water through the reeds, like little frogs hurrying through grass from the advance of a man, or running to and fro in utter dismay on the towing-path.

Then suddenly the white flashes of the heat-ray came leaping towards me. The houses caved in as they dissolved at its touch, and darted out flames; the trees changed to fire with a roar. It flickered up and down the towing-path, licking off the people who ran this way and that, and came down to the water's edge not fifty yards from where I stood. It swept across the river to Shepperton, and the water in its track rose in a boiling wheal crested with steam. I turned shoreward.

In another moment the huge wave, well-nigh at the boiling-point, had rushed upon me. I screamed aloud, and, scalded, half-blinded, agonized, I staggered through the leaping, hissing water towards the shore. Had my feet stumbled, it would have been the end. I fell helplessly, in full sight of the Martians, upon the broad, bare gravelly spit that runs down to mark the angle of the Wey and Thames. I expected nothing but death. I have a dim memory of the foot of a Martian coming down within a score of feet of my head, driving straight into the loose gravel, whirling it this way and that, and lifting again; of a long suspense, and then of the four carrying the *débris* of their comrade between them, now clear, and then presently faint, through a veil of smoke, receding interminably, as it seemed to me, across a vast space of river and meadow. And then, very slowly, I realized that by a miracle I had escaped.

But it was not on the heat-ray that the Martians chiefly relied in their march on London. The monsters I saw that evening as I fled were armed with tubes which they discharged like guns. There was no flash, no smoke, simply that loaded detonation.

Every minute I expected the fire of some hidden battery to spring upon them, but the evening calm was unbroken. Their figures grew smaller as they receded, and presently the gathering night had swallowed them up. Only towards Sunbury was a dark appearance, as though a conical hill had suddenly come into being there, and remoter across the river, towards Walton, I saw another such summit. They grew lower and broader even as I stared. These, as I knew later, were the black smoke. It was heavy, this vapour, heavier than the densest smoke, so that, after the first tumultuous uprush and outflow of its impact, it sank down through the air and poured over the ground in a manner rather liquid than gaseous, abandoning the hills, and streaming into the valleys and ditches and watercourses, even as I have heard the carbonic acid gas that pours from volcanic clefts is wont to do. And the touch of that vapour, the inhaling of its pungent wisps, was death to all that breathes.

One has to imagine the fate of those batteries towards Esher, waiting so tensely in the twilight, as well as one may. Survivors there were none. One may picture the orderly expectation, the officers alert and watchful, the gunners ready, the ammunition piled to hand, the limber gunners with their horses and wagons, the groups of civilian spectators standing as near as they were permitted, the evening stillness, the ambulances and hospital tents, with the burnt and wounded from Weybridge; then the dull resonance of the shots the Martians fired, and the clumsy projectile whirling over the trees and houses, and smashing amidst the neighbouring fields.

One may picture, too, the sudden shifting of the attention, the swiftly spreading coils and bellyings of that blackness advancing headlong, towering heavenward, turning the twilight to a palpable darkness, a strange and horrible antagonist of vapour striding upon its victims, men and horses near it seen dimly running, shrieking, falling headlong, shouts of dismay, the guns suddenly abandoned, men choking and writhing on the ground, and the swift broadening out of the opaque cone of smoke. And then, night and extinction – nothing but a silent mass of impenetrable vapour hiding its dead.

III

DEAD LONDON

So you understand the roaring wave of fear that swept through the greatest city in the world just as Monday was dawning – the stream of flight rising swiftly to a torrent, lashing in a foaming tumult round the railway stations, banked up into a horrible struggle about the shipping in the Thames, and hurrying by every available channel northward and eastward. By ten o'clock the police organization, and by midday even the railway organizations, were losing coherency, losing shape and efficiency, guttering, softening, running at last in that swift liquefaction of the social body.

All the railway lines north of the Thames and the South-Eastern people at Cannon Street had been warned by midnight on Sunday, and trains were being filled, people were fighting savagely for standing-room in the carriages, even at two o'clock. By three people were being trampled and crushed even in Bishopsgate Street; a couple of hundred yards or more from Liverpool Street station revolvers were fired, people stabbed, and the policemen who had been sent to direct the traffic, exhausted and infuriated, were breaking the heads of the people they were called out to protect.

And as the day advanced the engine-drivers and stokers refused to return to London, the pressure of the flight drove the people in an ever-thickening multitude away from the stations and along the northward-running roads. By midday a Martian had been seen at Barnes, and a cloud of slowly sinking black vapour drove along the Thames and across the flats of Lambeth, cutting off all escape over the bridges in its advance.

If one could have hung that June morning in a balloon in the blazing blue above London, every northward and eastward road running out of the infinite tangle of streets would have seemed stippled black with the streaming fugitives, each dot a human agony of terror and physical distress.

Directly below him the balloonist would have seen the

network of streets far and wide, houses, churches, squares, crescents, gardens – already derelict – spread out like a huge map, and in the southward *blotted*. Over Ealing, Richmond, Wimbledon, it would have seemed as if some monstrous pen had flung ink upon the chart. Steadily, incessantly, each black splash grew and spread, shooting out ramifications this way and that, now banking itself against rising ground, now pouring swiftly over a crest into a new-found valley, exactly as a gout of ink would spread itself upon blotting-paper.

And beyond, over the blue hills that rise southward of the river, the glittering Martians went to and fro, calmly and methodically spreading their poison-cloud over this patch of country, and then over that, laying it again with their steam-jets when it had served its purpose, and taking possession of the conquered country. They do not seem to have aimed at extermination so much as at complete demoralization and the destruction of any opposition. They exploded any stores of powder they came upon, cut every telegraph, and wrecked the railways here and there. They were hamstringing mankind. They seemed in no hurry to extend the field of operations, and they did not come beyond the central part of London all that day. It is possible that a very considerable number of people in London stuck to their houses through Monday morning. Certain it is that many died at home, suffocated by the black smoke.

I have not space here to tell you of my adventures during the days that followed – of how I saw men caught for the Martians' food, of how the third falling star smashed the house where I was resting, and of what I saw while I was hiding there. When I came out into the air again I found about me the landscape, weird and lurid, of another planet. Everywhere spread the red weed, whose seed the Martians had brought with them. All round were red cactus-shaped plants, knee-high, without a solitary terrestrial growth to dispute their footing. The trees near me were dead and brown, but further, a network of red threads scaled the still living stems. I went on my way to Hampstead through scarlet and crimson trees; it was like walking through an avenue of gigantic blood-drops.

IV

HOW THE MARTIANS WERE SLAIN

It was near South Kensington that I first heard the howling. It crept almost imperceptibly upon my senses. It was a sobbing alternation of two notes, 'Ulla, ulla, ulla, ulla,' keeping on perpetually. I stopped, wondering at this strange, remote wailing. It was as if that mighty desert of houses had found a voice for its fear and solitude. It was not until I emerged from Baker Street that I saw, far away over the trees in the clearness of the sunset, the hood of the Martian giant from which this howling proceeded. I watched him for some time, but he did not move.

I came upon the wrecked handling machine halfway to St John's Wood Station. At first I thought a house had fallen across the road. It was only as I clambered among the ruins that I saw, with a start, this mechanical Samson lying, with its tentacles bent and smashed and twisted, among the ruins it had made. The fore part was shattered. It seemed as if it had driven blindly straight at the house, and had been overwhelmed in its overthrow.

A little beyond the ruins about the smashed handling machine I came upon the red weed again, and found Regent's Canal a spongy mass of dark red vegetation.

The dusky houses about me stood faint and tall and dim; the trees towards the park were growing black. All about me the red weed clambered among the ruins, writhing to get above me in the dim. Night, the mother of fear and mystery, was coming upon me. London gazed at me spectrally. The windows in the white houses were like the eye-sockets of skulls. About me my imagination found a thousand noiseless enemies moving. Terror seized me, a horror of my temerity. Far away, I saw a second Martian, motionless as the first, standing in the park towards the Zoological Gardens, and silent.

An insane resolve possessed me. I would die and end it. And I would save myself even the trouble of killing myself. I marched on recklessly towards this Titan, and then, as I drew nearer and the light grew, I saw that a multitude of black birds was circling and clustering about the hood. At that my heart gave a bound, and I began running along the road. Great mounds had been heaped about the crest of the hill, making a huge redoubt of it. It was the final and largest place the Martians made. And from behind these heaps there rose a thin smoke against the sky. Against the skyline an eager dog ran and disappeared. The thought that had flashed into my mind grew real, grew credible. I felt no fear, only a wild, trembling exultation, as I ran up the hill towards the motionless monster. Out of the hood hung lank shreds of brown at which the hungry birds pecked and tore.

In another moment I had scrambled up the earthen rampart and stood upon its crest, and the interior of the redoubt was below me. A mighty space it was, with gigantic machines here and there within it, huge mounds of material and strange shelter places. And, scattered about it, some in their overturned war-machines, some in the now rigid handling machines, and a dozen of them stark and silent and laid in a row, were the Martians – *dead!* – slain by the putrefactive and disease bacteria against which their systems were unprepared; slain as the red weed was being slain; slain, after all man's devices had failed, by the humblest things that God, in His wisdom, had put upon this earth.

Already when I watched them they were irrevocably doomed, dying and rotting even as they went to and fro. It was inevitable. By the toll of a billion deaths man has bought his birthright of the earth, and it is his against all comers; it would still be his were the Martians ten times as mighty as they are. For neither do men live nor die in vain.

II

Terror from the Sea

Eden Phillpotts

Though 'The Invasion From Mars' remains the most famous 'panic'
radio broadcast, it was actually not the first to create genuine fear among
its listeners. This distinction belongs to a British production which
preceded Orson Welles' show by just two months. The story was called
'Terror From The Sea' and it was aired by the BBC on 20 August,
1938. Here, too, the producer, Cyril Wood, had dramatised a story by
the prolific fantasy writer Eden Phillpotts in such a way that some
listeners believed they were hearing details of a new species of huge crabs
which had emerged from the depths of the ocean to terrorise mankind.
Originally written two years earlier in 1936, the work had been rather
prosaically called 'The Owl of the Athene'. However, although the
scriptwriter, Froom Tyler, did not employ the out-and-out 'news
bulletin' style of his American counterpart, so vivid was his adaptation
that it caused 'a small-scale scare akin to the panic later generated by the
Mercury Theatre in the USA', according to SF authority Brian
Stableford. Some splendidly convincing characterisation by radio actors
Ralph Truman, Roy Baker, Brenda Grossmith and a young Jack Train
also helped create an illusion of believability that had listeners ringing
both the BBC and the police about what they thought was an invasion of
the Devon coast by huge crustacians. The author, Eden Phillpotts,
(1862-1960) was, of course, a West Countryman, and cunningly set
his tale in an area with which he was intimately acquainted. He also
knew that the sea here does genuinely throw up some of the largest crabs
to be found in the British Isles. (It was also, incidentally, most
appropriate that the story should be set in Weston-Super-Mare, for it
had been here in 1896 that Marconi had established the first
transmission and reception of radio waves with distant Penarth in

26

*Glamorgan.) This said, one can imagine just how the story which follows
had more than a little ring of the possible about it ...*

One August morning a West of England newspaper printed the
following paragraphs in its columns:

'Since alcohol was banished from our tables and may no
longer be drunk save under medical prescription, feats of
imagination are not so common and do not win the respectful
attention our ancestors were wont to give them; but of old,
familiar spectres were accustomed to appear in the newspaper,
when news ran short, and the Sea Serpent and Great
Gooseberry usually adorned our pages during the holiday
season. Imagination, however, being a thing of the past and
flights of fancy long since relegated to the nursery, it is
somewhat astounding to be reminded of these ancient
aberrations at the present day. Old men no longer see visions,
nor do young men dream dreams, so what shall be said of this
preposterous story from a Devon strand? Whence its
inspiration and how comes it that not less than five adult
human beings stoutly cleave to it despite the laughter of their
neighbours?

'Long-shore fisherfolk they are, who have their business in
shallow waters with hook and line, net and lobster-pot. They
operate from a strip of sand dunes and waste land a mile long
which separates the estuarial waters of the river Exe from the sea
and is known as Dawlish Warren. When men of old played ball
games, golf links occupied this region; to-day it is derelict.

'Descending through these sand dunes at dawn to their boat,
which lay upon the beach awaiting them, the fishers emerged
upon the shore under the first grey of a still and cloudy
morning. Light was as yet very dim, but the eastern sky began
to mantle. Suddenly they saw a huge blot rising at the junction
of sea and shore. It loomed large and dark against the peaceful
dawn behind it and suggested to them the possibility that some
small sloop, or coasting vessel, had lost her bearings and run
aground by night.

'They were hastening to her when the keenest-eyed of the
party stayed his mates and, as they all allege, saved their lives
by doing so. The mass had moved. They stood still and, the
light increasing, made a tremendous discovery. This great

object at sea-level was alive, and the horrified spectators perceived that a marine crab confronted them. It resembled those they daily caught – the edible crab of commerce; but it was as large as an army tank, and they judged it must have weighed five hundred tons or more. Appalled and doubting their senses, the good fellows retreated backwards; but the monster had observed them. They declare that its large, black eyes were poised upon protruding stalks three feet long and moved in waving fashion to right and left as a flower blown by the wind upon its stem. They stood now two hundred yards from the creature, but it was evidently aware of their presence, and our sailormen declare, as the next item in this nightmare, that from the shell of the crustacean above its head (if indeed crabs possess anything to be called a head) there shot suddenly a puff of vapour, as though a gas gun had been fired. And this was indeed what had happened! The crab had directed his discharge at them and a moment later they became conscious of the fact. The morning air grew thick with a heavy odour that none had ever known until then, and they ran away from it as fast as they might. One man fainted and his companions picked him up and continued their combined retreat into purer atmosphere. The sufferer swiftly returned to consciousness and the air about them grew sweet again. Their restricted breathing was restored and none suffered any ill effects from the discharge; but all are confident that, had they been nearer the giant, they must have perished. For a time they feared pursuit, but nothing further happened and, as dawn waxed and the light of day brightened the dunes, two of the fishermen crept back to the shore and, concealing themselves behind a ridge of sand and bent grass, spied upon the beach. They were just in time to see an upheaval of the sea and mark a disturbance of the placid tide as the intruder returned to its element. They waited an hour, saw no more of it and presently, with what appears to us considerable courage, launched their boat and went about their business.

'It seems that they debated their weird experience and naturally hesitated to tell it; but since no less than five men were agreed as to the details of the adventure, it appeared to them worthy of credence.

'As our representative has conveyed this narrative to

Professor Macmurdoch, principal of the great Marine Laboratory at Plymouth and the first living authority on the Crustacea, we are enabled to conclude our singular story with the learned gentleman's comment upon it.

' "That there are far larger decapods in the sea than ever came out of it," he admitted, "is exceedingly probable. Indeed submarine exploration has revealed their existence and at a mile beneath the surface of temperate and tropical oceans our diving chambers have reported the spider crab as large as a man, and often larger. It is not impossible that in those three-mile depths of the sea, as yet inadequately explored, there may dwell enormous crustaceans lighted, as are the deep sea fish, by their own electricity and created to resist the terrific weight of water above them. Science can offer no objections to such a possibility; but a crab weighing five hundred tons and armed with a gas gun upon his carapace must certainly be seen before it can be credited, and I for one should feel quite unprepared to accept the testimony of five mariners, or even five hundred. Such a chimera belongs to the days of fiction, when our forefathers still won pleasure from myth and legend, and human imagination played with fact, finding childish amusement in peopling the world with ogres and fairies and reading all manner of fanciful inventions, together with poetry and romance. But that time is past; fiction has disappeared; and the only interesting thing about this absurdity would be to learn by what trick, or freak of atavism, these simple fellows should have concocted or imagined such a piece of nonsense. That a solitary sailor of weak mind might have shown his ancient ancestry in this fashion, by imagining the thing that is not, one could easily understand; but that five fishermen tell the same story can, I fear, only be explained in one way. They desire to gain a little attention and possibly some pecuniary advantage from the tale. They have invented a new 'Rhyme of the Ancient Mariner'; and if you ask me what that might be, I shall tell you that it is a piece of poetry written in remote time by a British bard, whose name I forget, though men of letters might possibly remember it.

' "To sum up," concluded the professor, "I think we may safely prophesy that we shall not hear of the Dawlish Warren crab again." '

But the expert proved mistaken, as experts are apt to be, and within one week of that Devonian experience, things began to happen that established the veracity of those English fishermen. Their little world had not done laughing at them before the world at large found itself faced with a growing problem of hideous complexity and the incursion of *Brychura Gigantea* began in earnest.

The great crab was reported from three places on the coast line of the Americas and from Newfoundland, while simultaneously solitary specimens appeared in South Africa, and on the African shore of the Red Sea. They occurred in the Yellow Sea also. One had visited Cyprus, another Malta, another Tripoli. The Baltic had seen them and Australia chronicled no less than nine upon her beaches. The accounts resembled each other and in one or two cases, supposing that the monsters were stranded by the tide, bodies of men had attacked them and perished under their poisonous discharge before the creatures returned unharmed to the sea. Only small arms had been employed on these occasions; but they failed to do any apparent injury.

The map of the world seemed to show that something like system and order attended the genesis of the crabs. Their pioneers and explorers were quartering out the earth, and a fact swiftly noted by science was this: that all seas appeared alike to them and they moved as freely in polar waters as around the temperate and tropical regions of ocean. The immediate objective was a capture, and Man assumed that so soon as he had slain or caught one of these formidable creatures, something as to its vulnerability might be learned. It was many weeks before actual fear appeared in the heart of humanity, together with those wild rumours and suspicions that fear is wont to breed; but anon a sense of real danger and doubt dawned before sensational news. In the Pacific something like concerted action began to be taken by Crab, and little groups of islands were overrun by it. The lowly inhabitants, hemmed in on all sides, for the most part perished and the majority of their small vessels were also destroyed, but survivors, who had put to sea and escaped, made land elsewhere and reported the fate of their clans and families. They painted hideous pictures of the ruin and death created; they vouched for it that Crab was a Man-eater and devoured his victims after he had slain them with dreadful emanations from himself.

Science, measuring the significance of these stories, accepted the truth of them since it became no longer possible to doubt. The chemists pondered the gas which Crab was able to exude and the naturalists doubted not that this vapour, when discharged under sea, would secure the creatures their prey of great fishes. But such an elastic fluid was far more volatile and clearly operated at a far greater range when shot into the air. Its constituents soon became a matter of vital interest.

Brychura Gigantea waxed in size and in numbers. His Pacific depredations swiftly increased, so that the 'wireless' daily recorded new successes for him and television from Fiji enabled Europe actually to see him at work. Samoa was overrun by a prodigious invasion and thousands of mankind perished under it; while many of those who thought to escape by water also lost their lives, for Crab now attacked shipping and the disappearance of considerable tonnage was recorded. Futile signals of distress sounded upon all the Seven Seas and fishing fleets were destroyed, sometimes without a survivor to tell the tale. The creatures could encircle a steam trawler with ease, drag it under the surface and sink it without a trace. No wooden ships now existed and, under motive power, the average speed of all craft great and small had much increased; but Crab when afloat was able to wreck all save armoured vessels by impact with his own carcase. The weight and speed of ships had enormously increased, however, and against modern tonnage of any size he was powerless save to offer his floating hordes against them, stay their progress and labour under sea to pierce their hulls.

Curious facts of natural history appeared and it was found that many small terrestrial species of the creatures, familiar to Man in the tropics and dwelling miles from the sea, were acting in unfamiliar fashion and operating in communion with their huge, marine compatriots. Observation revealed a connection, though its character could not be understood; but when the land crabs began to leave their mountain haunts and swarm seawards, many unhappy islanders knew that their turn had come. The sign could not be mistaken or the warning disregarded. In the West Indies thousands of white and coloured people were thus able to leave their homes by sea in time and reach Barbados, Jamaica and the larger islands now arming against incursion.

From these phenomena arose a dreadful theory that Crab was revealing something more than instinct, and science divided into two camps upon this question, the one holding that a measure of reason marked his operations, the other protesting against any hypothesis so terrible from a human standpoint, and declaring that *Brychura* operated mechanically and had only been drawn from the depths to seek unfamiliar light and air by some sudden accident of increase which multiplied his species abnormally. In any case no possibility existed of communicating with the creatures, or reaching such intelligence and comprehension as they might possess. No link could be forged and Man now perceived that death was the sole weapon to be used against them. But Crab increased by millions and his destruction in huge numbers, when compassed by explosives from the air, deterred him not at all. The danger zones widened; he increased his grip from the islands to the main lands; he penetrated the great river estuaries of North and South America; India and China began to swarm with him. At a thousand points, from North to South and upon every continent, Man found himself steadily driven back, and when fleets of bombing airplanes broke the crustacean ranks and slaughtered oncoming hosts, fresh legions surged out of the sea to devour their fallen and trample with hideous deliberation forward into all lands. Where individual pioneers from the horde had early been cut off and killed, Man was able to examine his foe scientifically and make important discoveries concerning his weapon and armour. The fighting lines had long been observed to consist of two species: the monstrous *Brychura* and the spider-crabs, their allies. The spiders were not larger, but far speedier, and they took the place of cavalry to the foot regiments of old. Spider Crab stood some twenty feet off the ground on lengthy legs as hard as steel and was the size of an average elephant. He could proceed over any sort of ground at forty miles an hour and he was responsible for appalling raids upon Man; but Spider proved more vulnerable than his massive companion, being as a cruiser to a battleship in naval terms.

Science discovered that the armour of the giant crabs was proof against anything but high explosives and of astounding and adamantine hardness. Nature had treated the lime of which it was composed to some formula beyond human ken and the substance of their skeletons could scarcely be scratched with anything less than diamond. Their gasometer was situated between the stalks of their eyes, with a sort of nozzle protruding beyond them and capable of being turned in any direction at the will of the operator. A cistern held the gas, which was created within the interior of the animal and stored in liquid form above. Chemistry analysed the constituents, and Man's history dated from that discovery the first ray of hope to shine through the darkness now crowding upon him.

Until this time no gas mask had proved able to resist the aerial poison distributed by Crab; while Man's counter-poisons ejected against the intruder had affected him not at all; but new experiments were made and defensive masks perfected, while meantime the great struggle continued under circumstances of increasing horror. Human hearts indeed were wrung to the limit, and thousands of men and women lost their senses, thousands committed suicide and slew their nearest and dearest as the remorseless monsters approached and no way of escape offered. Crab's numbers continued to be incalculable and the death of thousands strewed the air of Earth with a new pestilence that took its toll before their advance.

But all men were already operating as one. Though he fouled the air, Crab could not stay the Herzian waves from their steadfast flow, and the world, thanks to wireless communication, had long since become but a little place. Closest concert of action was therefore possible between her kingdoms; immense speeds were long since attained in air, and the great flying ships of all peoples flew at a thousand miles an hour. Thus concentrations against Crab became possible, and East and West, North and South, wherever Man suffered and fought, were closely linked in speech and understanding. The greatest sea vessels were also immune, and where Crab had proceeded, like the hordes of the locust, to destroy human food upon his march, the ranks of depleted men were succoured when possible from the ends of Earth.

The fighting technique of Crab did not improve and huge reverses failed to sharpen his instincts. Over many districts of Earth the unconscious monsters gave themselves into the hands of Man since their method of operations brought them in masses against his barriers and it became possible to destroy them in immense numbers from the air. Every seaside town and port was protected so far as it might be done, but vast tracts of continental coast had been conquered by the enemy and from these strongholds he swarmed inland. Crab, however, lacked method and knew no means of commissariat. His pioneers plodded everywhere slaying and devouring, but thousands perished in the great deserts of Arabia and North Africa, where for generations afterwards their stony skeletons persisted – a perch for vulture and rendezvous for jackal – until the simoon hid them beneath the sand for ever. Some reaching great oases, wherein no power existed to oppose them, slew the inhabitants and laid the fertile regions waste.

The Foreign Legion battled with them but was worsted, for their terrible encounters had occurred before the gas mask came into being that could resist Crab. And still they gathered from the seas until many great islands had fallen; Greenland was gone with Iceland, Newfoundland promised soon to succumb. Air-planes now of huge size carried the inhabitants of many lost regions into safety and the conscious world was one, working with sole purpose to save dwindling humanity against the scourge. Thousands of young men found their life's work in the air and inflicted gigantic losses upon the enemy. A phenomenon appeared on the far flung battle front, for it seemed that a sort of reason did, after all, animate and direct Crab. He, too, acknowledged leaders and, in the third year of the attempted conquest, crustaceans of fabulous size came to the shore as commanders of the hosts, and about them the rank and file assembled. Man concentrated against these colossi – creatures that towered into the air like pyramids – and a fierce attack did shattering injury to one, where it had heaved up in the delta of Nile near Alexandria. But its companions crowded about it and the wounded mass was supported and conveyed into the Mediterranean beyond reach of further harm.

Man built a new submarine, for Crab was able to encompass

and destroy the old type. But with a small and mobile vessel of immense resisting strength, heroes plumbed the depths and carried death to Crab in his own element. Exploratory work of these under-sea ships continued to report enormous reserves awaiting their turn to march upon Earth, and described creatures as great as the British cathedral of St Paul operating beneath.

Science suspected that a new genesis of Crab had occurred and, as the queen bee pours forth endless streams of life, so now Man's enemy must be breeding with a fecund profusion that no opposing forces were ever likely to limit.

Meantime the whole trend and purpose of human life became perforce changed and there was built a close intercommunion that brooked no interference of any sort. Such unsocial spirits as strove to benefit from the appalling crisis, or pluck personal advantage out of it, were destroyed and swept from humanity's path. The tangled business of commerce, the confusions of monetary exchange, the thousand cumbrous and intricate barriers that Man had raised between himself and his brother were swept into the melting pot. No longer might the secure make hard terms with those in peril; no longer might neutral nations stand at gaze and profit from the sufferings of their fellows. There was none secure, no neutrals to bargain, no kingdoms beyond reach of Crab.

Night and day were alike to the invader. He carried light with him; his huge, stalked eyes could see in the dark, and Man's flood-lighting showed the monsters trudging by thousands inland – ever inland – through the hours of night. The loss to humanity far transcended any computation and the race was beggared before the end. Beleaguered, surrounded, steadily driven in upon his great protected cities and lesser towns, he saw the work of his hands cast down and many monuments of art and industry destroyed.

Canada and the Americas began to lose heart at the beginning of the third year, for Crab had now penetrated to the Great Lakes and from them issued in mighty force both North and South. Out of the tropic regions of Brazil, from the Amazon and Orinoco, hordes poured North to join forces by way of Panama and Mexico; while the frontier State of Maine in the United States afforded, through its network of estuaries and great meres, abundant support and was in the enemy's claws. Japan and Australia were lost at this season also.

A tiny islet upon the western borders of Europe had long excited the admiration of Earth by the strength of its resistance, and now, nearly at its last gasp, from this little kingdom of the British Isles, a pharmaceutical chemist's assistant by name of Albert Mugg, emerged into the limelight of history and wakened new hope for his kind.

His discovery was by no means entirely responsible for a turn in the desperate affairs of Man, but it synchronised with other events and helped to reawaken hope long foundered. There is no doubt that, inspired by a passionate patriotism and devotion to his country, Albert Mugg sacrificed his own life to its preservation without any more extended ambition; but Earth was at a crisis when to save one nation from the onset was to hearten and help them all, and his discovery, probably animated by no grander desire than to rescue his native town from destruction, may be said to represent a tremendous and vital moment of the terrestrial conflict. He came from what was known as a fashionable watering-place of little moment, but his ancestors had dwelt here, his life was spent here; he possessed a wife and two children; and their home and welfare roused in this pharmaceutical chemist such a passionate genius that he devised means for the protection and release of Weston-Super-Mare from the adamant legions now closing in upon it. Germs without number had, indeed, already been scattered over Crab and every poison known as fatal to Man and beast pressed upon him without visible effect; but Albert Mugg, after numberless experiments, hit upon a combination and implored the local authority to let an experiment be made with it. Many flying machines were protecting the neighbouring city of Bristol, which was also sore beset, but there were none just then available at Weston and the whole question of aerial defence began to grow more and more impossible for Man. He still flew with petrol fuel and the supply was rapidly giving out. Already the demand far exceeded it and he was called to employ the spirit with infinite precautions.

An appeal, however, met with swift response, and a gyroscope appeared, landed in safety and ascended again with Mugg and his apparatus. It was simple enough and consisted of a gardener's syringe and a pail of chemicals. Mugg's inspiration arose from the conviction that in one spot alone Crab must prove vulnerable, and he suspected that if a poison could enter *Brychura*'s eye it would not only blind him but proceed through this channel to the enemy's brain and cause swift destruction. What was of no avail upon his armoured body might prove all-powerful if directed against the ebon eyes, that moved upon their stalks like huge black poppies above every enemy's head and directed its vision where it willed.

A great opportunity was offered to Mugg and his airman, for amid the encircling host that now only awaited nightfall for successful attack upon the little town, there towered one of the monsters – a spider crab so huge that he resembled the edifice of some insane architect and rose upon vast shanks to the height of the Eiffel Tower. This enormous thing was a leader and the centre of an army.

With courage won from a thousand encounters, the pilot launched Albert upon his ordeal, flew steadily at a height of five hundred feet above the giant, then, like a bird of prey, hovered in air and slowly sank until the creature beneath was in range. It lifted a prodigious claw above its head and ejected a spurt of venom upwards; but the airman had long learned how to keep out of danger and his mask made him safe enough. He poised at a height of fifty feet above the agitated giant beneath. Its eyes were pointed upwards now – black, lustrous circles with a diameter of a yard – and Mugg, filling his syringe and waiting for the sudden dart and swoop of the machine, discharged his metallic concoction full and fair into each of the great orbs uplifted upon him. Then the pilot mounted and stood off, while twenty thousand people behind the protections of Weston waited to behold what might come of their fellow townsman's experiment.

A stupendous spectacle rewarded them. When struck by high explosive Crab generally perished instantly, for a shattered carapace meant death. At a successful impact he tucked in his pincers and ceased to live. The mighty creature now stricken acted otherwise. No sound emerged from it, but the great erection tottered, its eyes, as though blasted, dropped helpless upon their stalks, it fell back supine and its legs rose into the air like a group of factory chimneys. The ground shook before this tremendous impact; but no motion followed until there rose a roar from watching human thousands. The mighty had fallen and probably the largest creature that Man had ever seen alive, he now saw dead. Crab, unable to understand the terrible fate which had overtaken his leader, stood for a moment helplessly staring into the sky and the air-plane swooped down again, while Albert once more operated upon the uplifted eyes beneath him until the last drop had fallen from his syringe. Ten more monsters met the discharge and incontinently perished. Then pilot and passenger returned to safety.

Within an hour Mugg's formula was despatched to the ends of the Earth and the genius himself had ceased to live, for his triumph brought death to a weakly frame and the chemist's heart was suddenly stilled by the thrill of joy awakened at his success.

Events of enormous significance quickly followed upon this local victory, and scientific observers, still watching and estimating every phase of Man's great challenge, were able to report that, for the first time, Crab's morale had been emphatically shaken by this reverse. Dimly but forcibly the monsters had perceived that Weston-Super-Mare possessed forces with which they could not reckon, and when night returned the expected struggle came not with it. There was only heard the ponderous din of Crab returning to the Severn Sea; and at dawn of day his dead alone remained in Somersetshire.

But Man was not yet quite at the end of his torment and the need for sleepless struggle still continued. Crab continued to hold on his dogged way and another mundane year of dire human tribulation needed to be faced and endured before the issue emerged without possibility of doubt.

For years after the great contest Crab still crept in lone valleys and amid the fastnesses of the lakes and mountains. He was hunted down as the wolf of old, and being now separated and scattered, only awaited discovery to meet his end. But the war was won and the beaten enemy at length conveyed his devastated hosts back again to the ocean. He lost many thousands more in the process, for the waves of every sea as they rolled in upon the land were now liberally drenched with metallic poison, and Crab found the gauntlet of the shallow waters hard to run. The crustaceans stood presently between two fatal forces, dying on shore and in every tide-way under the malign application of 'Albert Mugg'. For no scientific and formidable name was ever given to the dead chemist's sublime synthesis. As 'Albert Mugg' it lived and the formula was preserved lest like peril should threaten Earth again.

So passed defeated Crab from the solid ground to his rightful and greater domain of the deep. No treaties or conferences marked the end of the encounter. Crab was not called to set his seal upon terms dictated by his conqueror; no demands impossible of fulfilment were heaped upon him; but memorials rose to commemorate the terrific event and every city and township of the least importance received a shell of Crab – to be set in their market places and central resorts for remembrance. Children played upon them and the herb of the field found foothold in their crannies, until they also disappeared, and *Brychura Gigantea* might only now be seen in his habit as he lived within the aisles of Earth's national museums.

III

The Diver

A.J.Alan

Radio stories which give listeners a pleasant thrill and even the occasional shudder were actually nothing new in the late 1930's, because one of the staple ingredients of broadcasting from its opening days in Britain in 1920 was the reading of tales of mystery and imagination. Indeed, the first specialist in this field was a certain A.J.Alan of whom the BBC's first Director-General, Lord Reith, was to speak of in these glowing terms in 1928: 'An old-time storyteller has found his way into the Twentieth Century from those days before the invention of printing when the art of storytelling was honoured by court, castle and cotter's ben,' he said. 'Until printing came to oust the storyteller from his place, the spoken word was all important – but now broadcasting has afforded the long-delayed opportunity for a revival. It is no exaggeration to say that A.J.Alan has been a pioneer. No storyteller before him ever had so many listeners; no listeners a better storyteller.' This man Alan was, in fact, almost as curious as the stories he told. His real name was Leslie Harrison Lambert (1883-1940) and he was the archetypal London man-about-town, working for the Foreign Office by day, and arriving at the BBC at night to broadcast wearing evening dress and sporting a monacle! He is also credited by radio authority Kenelm Foss with having originated that distinctive BBC accent 'a class-conscious mincing tradition of correct diction'. Certainly A.J.Alan told his monologues in a distinctive, idiosyncratic and sometimes gently self-mocking style, but listeners undoubtedly delighted in his self-written tales which ranged from the sardonic to the supernatural. There is, I think, no better example of Alan at work than this story, 'The Diver', which gives a vivid impression of his style and the way he absorbed his unseen audience into a story of the uncanny. It is not hard to imagine

40

that distinctive voice crackling over the air waves with his invariable greeting, 'Good evening, everyone!' as you read what follows.

For some reason or other the BBC are always asking me to tell a ghost story – at least, they don't ask me, they tell me I've got to. I say, 'What kind of a ghost story?' and they say, 'Any kind you like, so long as it's a personal experience and perfectly true.'

Just like that; and it's cramped my style a bit. Not that my personal experiences aren't true. Please don't think that. But it's simply this: that when it comes to supernatural matters my luck hasn't been very good. It isn't that I don't believe in such things on principle, but I do like to be present when the manifestations actually occur, instead of just taking other people's word for them; and, somehow or other, as I've said before, my luck has not been very good.

Lots of people have tried to convert me. There was one young woman in particular. She took a lot of trouble about it – quite a lot. She used to dra – take me to all sorts of parties where they had séances – you know the kind: table-turning, planchette, and so on – but it wasn't any good. Nothing ever happened when I was there. Nothing spiritual, that is. People always said:

'Ah, my boy, you ought to have been here last night. The table fairly got up and hit us in the face.'

Possibly very wonderful – but, after all, the ground will do that if you let it.

Well, as I say, they took me to several of these parties, and we used to sit for hours round tables, in a dim light, holding hands. That was rather fun sometimes – it depended on who one sat next to – but apart from that, the nights they took me, no manifestations ever occurred. Planchette wouldn't spell a word, and the table might have been screwed to the floor. To begin with they used to put it down to chance, or the conditions not being favourable. But after a time they began to put it down to me – and I thought: 'Something will have to be done about it.' It's never amusing to be looked upon as a sort of Jonah.

So I invented a patent table-tapper. It was made on the same principle as lazy tongs. You held it between your knees, and when you squeezed it a little mallet shot up (it was really a cotton reel stuck on the end of a pencil) and it hit the underneath of the table a proper biff. It was worked entirely with the knees, so that I could still hold the hands of the people on either side of me. And it was a success from the word 'Go'.

At the very next séance, as soon as the lights were down, I gave just a gentle tap. Our host said:

'Ah, a powerful force is present!' and I gave a louder – ponk! Then he said:

'How do you say "Yes"?' – and I said:

'Ponk!' Then he said:

'How do you say "No"?' And I said:

'Ponk, ponk!'

So far so good. Communication established. Then people began asking questions and I spelt out the answers. Awful hard work ponking right through the alphabet, but quite worth it. I'm afraid some of my answers made people sit up a bit. They got quite nervous as to what was coming next. Needless to say, this was some years ago.

Then someone said:

'Who's going to win the Derby?' (I don't know *who* said that) and I laboriously spelt out Signorinetta. This was two days before the race. I don't know *why* I said Signorinetta, because there were several horses with shorter names, but it just came into my head. The annoying thing was that I didn't take my own tip and back it. You may remember it won at 100 to 1 by I don't know how many lengths – five lengths dividing second and third. However, it's no use crying over the stable door after the horse has spilt the milk, and it has nothing whatever to do with the story.

The amusing thing was that when the séance was over various people came round to me and said:

'*Now* will you believe in spiritualism?' 'What more proof do you want?' and so on and so forth. It struck me as rather rich that they should try to convert me with my own false evidence. And I don't mind betting you that if I'd owned up to the whole thing being a spoof, not a soul would have believed me. That's always the way.

I've told you all this to show that I'm not exactly dippy on the subject of spiritualism – at any rate, not the table-turning variety – very largely because it *is* so easy to fake your results.

But when something *genuinely* uncanny comes along – why, then I'm one of the very first to be duly thrilled and mystified and – what not. It's one of those *genuine* cases I want to tell you about. It happened to me personally. But first of all you must know that there's a swimming bath at my club. Very good swimming bath, too. Deep at one end and shallow at the other. There's a sort of hall-place adjoining it, and in this hall there's a sandwich bar – very popular. It's much cheaper than lunching upstairs. Quite a lot of people seem to gravitate down there – especially towards the end of the month. Everything's quite informal. You just go to the counter and snatch what you want and take it to a table and eat it. Then when you've done, you go and tell George what you've had. George runs the show, and he says 'one-and-ninepence', or whatever it is, and that's that.

Personally, I usually go to a table in a little recess close to the edge of the swimming bath itself. You have to go down a few steps to get to it. But you are rather out of the turmoil and not so likely to get anything spilt over you. It's quite dangerous sometimes, people darting in and out like a lot of sharks – which reminds me: a member once wrote in to the secretary complaining that the place wasn't safe – I shan't say who it was, but you'd know his name if I told you; I managed to get hold of a copy of his letter. This is what he says, speaking of the sandwich bar:

'I once saw an enormous shark, at least five feet ten inches long, go up to the counter and seize a sausage roll – itself nearly four inches long – and take it away to devour it. When he had bitten off the end, which he did with a single snap of his powerful jaws, he found that it was empty. The sausage, which ought to have been inside, had completely vanished. It had been stolen by another shark even more voracious and ferocious than himself.

'Never shall I forget the awful spectacle of the baffled and impotent rage of this fearful monster. He went back to the counter, taking the empty sarcophagus with him, and said: "George, I have been stung!"

'In order to avoid such scenes of unparalleled and revolting cruelty' – after that he is rather inclined to exaggerate, so I shan't read any more – I usually go late, when the rush is over and it's fairly quiet. People come and practise diving, and sometimes they are worth watching – and sometimes not.

That's the sort of place it is, and if you know of anywhere less likely to be haunted I should like to see it. Very well, then.

One day I was just finishing lunch when there was a splash. I was reading a letter and didn't look up at once, but when I did I was rather surprised to see no ripples on the water, and no one swimming about, so I went on with my letter and didn't think any more about it. That was all that happened that day.

Two or three weeks later, at about the same time, I was again finishing lunch, and there was another splash. This time I looked up almost at once and saw the ripples, and it struck me *then* that it must have been an extraordinarily clean dive, considering that whoever it was must have gone in off the top. One could tell that from where the ripples were – well out in the middle. So I waited for him to come up. But he didn't come up. Then I thought that he must be doing a length under water, and I got up and went to the edge of the bath to watch for him. But still he didn't come up and I got a bit worried. He might have bumped his head on the bottom, or fainted, or anything, and I saw myself having to go in after him with all my clothes on.

I sprinted right round the bath, but there was undoubtedly no one in it. The attendant came out of one of the dressing-rooms and evidently thought I'd gone cracked, so I went to the weighing-machine and weighed myself – eleven stone eight – but I don't think he believed me.

That was the second incident. The third came about a fortnight later. This time I saw the whole thing clearly. I was sitting at my usual table and I saw a man climbing up the ladder leading to the top diving-board. When he got up there he came out to the extreme end of the plank and stood for a few seconds rubbing his chest and so on – like people often do.

He was rather tall and muscular – dark, with a small moustache – but what particularly caught my eye was a great big scar he had. It was about nine inches long and it reached down from his left shoulder towards the middle of his chest. It looked like a bad gash with a bayonet. It must have hurt quite a lot when it was done.

I don't know why I took so much notice of him, but I just did, that's all. And, funnily enough, he seemed to be just as much interested in me as I was in him. He gave me a most meaningful look. I didn't know what it meant, but it was undoubtedly a meaningful look.

As soon as he saw that he'd got me watching him he dived in, and it was the most gorgeous dive I've ever seen. Hardly any noise or splash – just a gentle sort of plop as though he'd gone into oil rather than water – and the ripples died away almost at once. I thought, if only he'll do that a few more times it'll teach me a lot, and I waited for him to come up – and waited – and waited – but not a sign.

I went to the edge of the bath, and then I walked right round it. But, bar the water, it was perfectly empty. However, to make absolutely certain – I mean that he couldn't have got out without my seeing him – I dug out the attendant and satisfied myself that no towels and – er – costumes had been given out since twelve o'clock – and it was then half-past two – and he, the attendant, he'd actually seen the last man leave.

The thing was getting quite serious. My scarred friend couldn't have melted away in the water, nor could he have dived slap through the bottom of the bath – at least, not without leaving some sort of a mark. So it was obvious that either the man had been a ghost, which was absurd – who's ever heard of a ghost in a swimming bath? – I mean the idea's too utterly – er – wet for anything – or that there was something wrong with the light lager I was having for lunch.

I went back to my table and found I'd hardly begun it, and in any case let me tell you it was *such* light lager that a gallon of it wouldn't have hurt a child of six – and – I'm *not* a child of six. So I ruled that out, and decided to wait and see if it happened again. It wouldn't have done to say anything about it. One's friends are apt to be a bit flippant when you tell 'em things like that. However, I made a point of sitting at the same table for weeks and weeks afterwards, but old stick-in-the-mud didn't show up again.

A good long time after this – it must have been eighteen months or more – I got an invitation to dine with some people called Pringle. They were old friends of mine, but I hadn't seen them for a long time because they'd mostly lived in Mexico, and one rather loses touch with people at that distance. Anyway, they were going back there in a few days, and this was a sort of farewell dinner.

They'd given up their flat and were staying at an hotel. They'd got another man dining with them. His name was Melhuish, and he was, with one exception, the most offensive blighter I've ever come across. Do you know those people who open their mouths to contradict what you are going to say before you've even begun to say it? Well, he did that, among other things. It was rather difficult to be entirely civil to him. He was travelling back to Mexico with the Pringles, as he'd got the job of manager to one of their properties. Something to do with oil, but I didn't quite grasp what, my mind was so taken up with trying to remember where on earth I'd seen the man before.

Of course *you* all know. You know he was the man who dived into the swimming bath. It sticks out about a mile, naturally; but I'd only seen him once before in a bad light, and it took me till half-way through the fish to place him. Then it came back with a rush, and my interest in him became very lively. He was an American, and he'd come over to England two months before, looking for a job – so he said. I asked him why he'd left America, and he didn't hear; but it did seem fairly certain that he'd never been in Europe before. So when we got to dessert I proceeded to drop my brick.

I said: 'Do you mind telling me whether you have a scar on your chest like this?' And I described it. The Pringles just stared, but Melhuish looked as if he were going to have a fit. Then he pulled himself together and said: 'Have you ever been in America?' And I said: 'No, not that I know of.' Then he said: 'Well, it's a most extraordinary thing, but I *have* a scar on my chest,' and he went on to explain how he'd got it.

Funnily enough, he'd gone in for high diving a lot when he was younger, and taken any amount of prizes, and on one occasion he'd found a sharp stake at the bottom ⌄i a river. He gave us full particulars. Very messy. But what they all wanted to know was how the – how I knew anything about it. Of course, it was a great temptation to tell 'em, but they'd only have thought I'd gone off my rocker, so I started a hare about perhaps having seen a photograph of his swimming club in some newspaper or other. They caught on to that idea quite well, so I left them to it.

The whole thing was by way of being rather a problem, and it kept me awake that night. Without being up in such matters, it did occur to me that it might be a warning of some kind. Is it likely that anyone – even a ghost – would take the trouble to come all the way from America simply to show me how well he could dive? Of course not, and I sort of thought that a man who was in the habit of going in off the deep end and *not* coming up again was no fit travelling companion for any friends of mine. I'm not superstitious, goodness knows! Of course, I don't walk under ladders, or light three matches with one cigarette, or any of those things, but that's because they're unlucky – not because I'm superstitious.

Anyhow, in case the Pringles might be, I went round next day and saw them. At least, I saw her – he was out – and told her all about the apparition at the club, and so on. That did it. She fairly went off pop. It was a portent, a direct intervention of Providence; nothing would induce her to travel with Melhuish after what she'd heard – and all the rest of it.

I left her to carry on the good work. I don't know how she managed it, but the fact remains that the Pringles did *not* start for Mexico, as arranged, and Melhuish did.

And now you are expecting me to say that the ship in which he sailed was never heard of again. But that wouldn't be strictly true. He got to the other side all right. But the train in which he was travelling through Mexico had to cross a bridge over a river. A steel bridge, it was. Now some months previously there'd been a slight scrap between two local bands of brigands, in the course of which the bridge had been blown up.

When the quarrel was patched up the bridge was patched up, too, but not with the meticulous care it might have been. The result was that in the daytime, when the sun was hot and the steelwork fully expanded, it was a perfectly good bridge, but at night, when it was cold and the girders had shrunk a bit – well, it didn't always quite meet in the middle.

It so happened that the train in question tried to cross this wretched bridge at the very moment when it was having rather a job to make both ends meet – and it simply couldn't bear it.

The middle span carried away and the engine and two carriages crashed through into the river, and fourteen people were killed. It was very sad about thirteen of them, but the fourteenth was Mr Melhuish.

There must be a moral to this story, if I could only think of it; but I can't, so perhaps some of you can help me by suggesting one ...

IV

The Tell-Tale Heart

Edgar Allan Poe

America, too, had its pioneer broadcaster of supernatural stories in the person of Raymond Edward Johnson who from the 1930's introduced the long-running CBS series, Inner Sanctum. *Once a week, Johnson would greet listeners with his distinctive and chilling tones: 'Good evening, friends. This is Raymond, your host, welcoming you in through the squeaking door to the Inner Sanctum. We have another tale to thrill you, and to chill you. Won't you come in and have a seat? No chair, you say? Why don't you try that black box over there? It's nice to have someone here who really believes in black magic, the supernatural, zombies and goblins. What's that? You don't really believe in those things? Well, our story tonight is about a man who didn't believe in them either. But he found out that he was wrong – dead wrong! Ha-ha-haaa ... ' Himan Brown, the producer, also played a major part in the success of the series by the lavish use of sound effects. He it was who devised the sound of a massive door creaking open which started every show: a sound which has since been patented! Brown actually found the creaking door prop quite by accident, but instantly realised its potential. He explains, 'I just thought it would be a marvellous way to start, with all its eeriness, and a sinister voice saying, "Come in!" But the actuality behind that voice is anybody's own creation. You create your own monster with the voice. That's what's so wonderful about radio.'* Inner Sanctum *attracted many famous actors and actresses and over the years adapted virtually every classic ghost and horror story. A favourite with Raymond Johnson and Himan Brown was an electrifying version of 'The Tell-Tale Heart' by Edgar Allan Poe which starred the great Boris Karloff. 'Poe wrote what is a beautiful radio script,' Brown commented years later. 'And the sound of that heart permeated*

49

everything, even driving the incomparable Karloff to higher octaves of terror.' What more suitable selection could there be, then, to represent Inner Sanctum *than Poe's masterpiece?*

True! – nervous – very, very dreadfully nervous I had been and am; but why *will* you say that I am mad? The disease had sharpened my senses – not destroyed – not dulled them. Above all was the sense of hearing acute. I heard all things in the heaven and in the earth. I heard many things in hell. How, then, am I mad? Hearken! and observe how healthily – how calmly I can tell you the whole story.

It is impossible to say how first the idea entered my brain; but once conceived, it haunted me day and night. Object there was none. Passion there was none. I loved the old man. He had never wronged me. He had never given me insult. For his gold I had no desire. I think it was his eye! yes, it was this! He had the eye of a vulture – a pale blue eye, with a film over it. Whenever it fell upon me, my blood ran cold; and so by degrees – very gradually – I made up my mind to take the life of the old man, and thus rid myself of the eye for ever.

Now this is the point. You fancy me mad. Madmen know nothing. But you should have seen *me*. You should have seen how wisely I proceeded – with what caution – with what foresight – with what dissimulation I went to work! I was never kinder to the old man than during the whole week before I killed him. And every night, about midnight, I turned the latch of his door and opened it – oh so gently! And then, when I had made an opening sufficient for my head, I put in a dark lantern, all closed, closed, so that no light shone out, and then I thrust in my head. Oh, you would have laughed to see how cunningly I thrust it in! I moved it slowly – very, very slowly, so that I might not disturb the old man's sleep. It took me an hour to place my whole head within the opening so far that I could see him as he lay upon his bed. Ha! – would a madman have been so wise as this? And then, when my head was well in the room, I undid the lantern cautiously – oh, so cautiously – cautiously (for the hinges creaked) – I undid it just so much that a single ray fell upon the vulture eye. And this I did for seven long nights – every night just at midnight – but I found the eye always closed; and so it was impossible to do the work;

for it was not the old man who vexed me, but his Evil Eye. And every morning, when the day broke, I went boldly into the chamber, and spoke courageously to him, calling him by name in a hearty tone, and inquiring how he had passed the night. So you see he would have been a very profound old man, indeed, to suspect that every night, just at twelve, I looked in upon him while he slept.

Upon the eighth night I was more than usually cautious in opening the door. A watch's minute hand moves more quickly than did mine. Never before that night, had I *felt* the extent of my own powers – of my sagacity. I could scarcely contain my feelings of triumph. To think that there I was, opening the door, little by little, and he not even to dream of my secret deeds or thoughts. I fairly chuckled at the idea; and perhaps he heard me; for he moved on the bed suddenly, as if startled. Now you may think that I drew back – but no. His room was as black as pitch with the thick darkness (for the shutters were close fastened, through fear of robbers), and so I knew that he could not see the opening of the door, and I kept pushing it on steadily, steadily.

I had my head in, and was about to open the lantern, when my thumb slipped upon the tin fastening, and the old man sprang up in bed, crying out – 'Who's there?'

I kept quite still and said nothing. For a whole hour I did not move a muscle, and in the meantime I did not hear him lie down. He was still sitting up in the bed listening; – just as I have done, night after night, hearkening to the death watches in the wall.

Presently I heard a slight groan, and I knew it was the groan of mortal terror. It was not a groan of pain or of grief – oh, no! – it was the low stifled sound that arises from the bottom of the soul when overcharged with awe. I knew the sound well. Many a night, just at midnight, when all the world slept, it has welled up from my own bosom, deepening, with its dreadful echo, the terrors that distracted me. I say I knew it well. I knew what the old man felt, and pitied him, although I chuckled at heart. I knew that he had been lying awake ever since the first slight noise, when he had turned in the bed. His fears had been ever since growing upon him. He had been trying to fancy them causeless, but could not. He had been saying to himself – 'It is nothing but the wind in the chimney – it is only a mouse crossing the floor', or 'it is merely a cricket which has made a single chirp.' Yes, he had been trying to comfort himself with these suppositions: but he had found all in vain. *All in vain*; because Death, in approaching him had stalked with his black shadow before him, and enveloped the victim. And it was the mournful influence of the unperceived shadow that caused him to feel – although he neither saw nor heard – to *feel* the presence of my head within the room.

When I had waited a long time, very patiently, without hearing him lie down, I resolved to open a little, a very, very little crevice in the lantern. So I opened it – you cannot imagine how stealthily, stealthily – until at length a single dim ray, like the thread of the spider, shot from out the crevice and fell full upon the vulture eye.

It was open – wide, wide open – and I grew furious as I gazed upon it. I saw it with perfect distinctness – all a dull blue, with a hideous veil over it that chilled the very marrow in my bones; but I could see nothing else of the old man's face or person: for I had directed the ray, as if by instinct, precisely upon the damned spot.

And have I not told you that what you mistake for madness is but over-acuteness of the senses? – now, I say, there came to my ears a low, dull, quick sound, such as a watch makes when enveloped in cotton. I knew *that* sound well, too. It was the beating of the old man's heart. It increased my fury, as the beating of a drum stimulates the soldier into courage.

But even yet I refrained and kept still. I scarcely breathed. I held the lantern motionless. I tried how steadily I could maintain the ray upon the eye. Meantime the hellish tattoo of the heart increased. It grew quicker and quicker, and louder and louder every instant. The old man's terror *must* have been extreme! It grew louder, I say, louder every moment! – do you mark me well? I have told you that I am nervous: so I am. And now at the dead hour of the night, amid the dreadful silence of that old house, so strange a noise as this excited me to uncontrollable terror. Yet, for some minutes longer I refrained and stood still. But the beating grew louder, louder! I thought the heart must burst. And now a new anxiety seized me – the sound would be heard by a neighbour! The old man's hour had come! With a loud yell, I threw open the lantern and leaped into the room. He shrieked once – once only. In an instant I dragged him to the floor, and pulled the heavy bed over him. I then smiled gaily, to find the deed so far done. But, for many minutes, the heart beat on with a muffled sound. This, however, did not vex me; it would not be heard through the wall. At length it ceased. The old man was dead. I removed the bed and examined the corpse. Yes, he was stone, stone dead. I placed my hand upon the heart and held it there many minutes. There was no pulsation. He was stone dead. His eye would trouble me no more.

If still you think me mad, you will think so no longer when I describe the wise precautions I took for the concealment of the body. The night waned, and I worked hastily, but in silence. First of all I dismembered the corpse. I cut off the head and the arms and the legs.

I then took up three planks from the flooring of the chamber, and deposited all between the scantlings. I then replaced the boards so cleverly, so cunningly, that no human eye – not even *his* – could have detected anything wrong. There was nothing to wash out – no stain of any kind – no blood-spot whatever. I had been too wary for that. A tub had caught all – ha! ha!

When I had made an end of these labours, it was four o'clock – still dark as midnight. As the bell sounded the hour, there came a knocking at the street door. I went down to open it with a light heart, – for what had I *now* to fear? There entered three men, who introduced themselves, with perfect suavity, as officers of the police. A shriek had been heard by a neighbour during the night; suspicion of foul play had been aroused; information had been lodged at the police office, and they (the officers) had been deputed to search the premises.

I smiled, – for *what* had I to fear? I bade the gentlemen welcome. The shriek, I said, was my own in a dream. The old man, I mentioned, was absent in the country. I took my visitors all over the house. I bade them search – search *well*. I led them, at length, to *his* chamber. I showed them his treasures, secure, undisturbed. In the enthusiasm of my confidence, I brought chairs into the room, and desired them *here* to rest from their fatigues, while I myself, in the wild audacity of my perfect triumph, placed my own seat upon the very spot beneath which reposed the corpse of my victim.

The officers were satisfied. My *manner* had convinced them. I was singularly at ease. They sat, and while I answered cheerily, they chatted of familiar things. But, ere long, I felt myself getting pale and wished them gone. My head ached, and I fancied a ringing in my ears: but still they sat and still chatted. The ringing became more distinct: – it continued and became more distinct: I talked more freely to get rid of the feeling: but it continued and gained definiteness – until, at length, I found that the noise was *not* within my ears.

No doubt I now grew *very* pale; – but I talked more fluently, and with a heightened voice. Yet the sound increased – and what could I do? It was *a low, dull quick sound – much such a sound as a watch makes when enveloped in cotton.* I gasped for breath – and yet the officers heard it not. I talked more quickly – more vehemently; but the noise steadily increased. I arose and argued about trifles, in a high key and with violent gesticulations; but the noise steadily increased. Why *would* they not be gone? I paced the floor to and fro with heavy strides, as if excited to fury by the observations of the men – but the noise steadily increased. Oh God! what *could* I do? I foamed – I raved – I swore! I swung the chair upon which I had been sitting, and grated it upon the boards, but the noise arose over all and continually increased. It grew louder – louder – *louder*! And still the men chatted pleasantly, and smiled. Was it possible they heard not? Almighty God! – no, no! They heard! – they suspected! – they *knew*! – they were making a mockery of my horror! – this I thought, and this I think. But anything was better than this agony! Anything was more tolerable than this derision! I could bear those hypocritical smiles no longer! I felt that I must scream or die! and now – again! – hark! louder! louder! louder! *louder!*

'Villains!' I shrieked, 'dissemble no more! I admit the deed! – tear up the planks! here, here! – it is the beating of his hideous heart!'

V

Incubus

Marjorie Bowen

The most successful series of supernatural stories broadcast by the BBC in the 1930's was probably Nightmares *which not only attracted a large and appreciative audience in the British Isles, but was equally well received when the stories of mystery and fear were repeated throughout the British Empire. The idea for the series had come from the Director-General Lord Reith – no doubt wishing to build on the success of A.J.Alan's broadcasts – and the production team recruited some of the best fantasy writers in the country to create original tales for the show. Among the top writers who contributed were Lady Cynthia Asquith, the former private secretary to J.M.Barrie and one of the foremost anthologists of macabre fiction; J.B.Moreton, better known as the* Daily Express *columnist, 'Beachcomber'; novelists H. de Vere Stackpole and Noel Streatfeild; the prodigiously talented Algernon Blackwood (soon to be a radio star himself) and the 'grand dame' of weird fiction, Marjorie Bowen, author of the classic novel* Black Magic *(1909) written when she was only in her early twenties. Miss Bowen (1886-1952) was an acknowledged expert on the supernatural – witchcraft and satanism in particular – and books like* The Devil Snar'd *(1933) and* The Bishop of Hell *(1949) as well as the aforementioned classic, have kept her memory alive to this day. For the series* Nightmares *she produced perhaps the most chilling of all the stories in 'Incubus' which I have much pleasure in returning to print here after a great many years in obscurity. It is an outstanding story in itself as well as being a splendid reminder of one of the BBC's best pre-war radio series.*

The guide said that it was very late in the year for visitors, but he allowed us to enter; the tall iron gate was slightly rusty and over it was a coloured statue with a starry crown. The sombre woods came down so close and thick to the garden wall that they seemed to be pressing into the walls and to be held back only by force.

This gloomy spot was, our guide said, hallowed; a heathen temple had stood there before the building of the monastery, and that was a long, long while ago. A deep restless curiosity had brought me to the place; I had been there for nights in succession in dreams, when the black forest had been flowing about me like waves and I had searched in vain for the walled vineyards, the long deserted buildings, the desecrated chantry with the echo, the church where the great wine butts stood.

It had been a sad journey through the mist, along the sodden ways, under the dark trees; the motion of the lopsided hired carriage had almost lulled me back into my dream; the road through the wood was very obscure owing to the blue-black leafage of the firs – the pale light over the monastery grounds seemed startling by contrast. The vintage was over and the place was desolate; the sullen guide clanked his keys and hunched his shoulders as he preceded us. I looked at my companions; they had no interest in the scene and seemed detached from it; I soon evaded them, leaving them standing, gaping, with their handbooks grasped in cold fingers, irresolute in the garth where the dry sticks of dead flowers thrust above the stagnant grass.

I was anxious to find some of the melancholy places familiar to me from my dreams; I heard the guide's voice calling after me peevishly, but took no heed as I hastened away down the cloisters. He was soon distanced, and I was free of the desolate covered walk. I found a poignant interest in noticing the difference between the reality and illusion; in my dream the place had been larger, but not more mournful, the forest had come down even closer, the façade of the long dwellings, the pillars of the cloisters had been interchangeable with the strong moist trunks of the trees, and the twisted undergrowth or shrub that was tangled into sombre recesses fit for a wild animal's lair.

I found a bitter satisfaction in confirming the solidity of my surroundings; the harsh walls were cold and damp to the touch, the cracked pavement rang beneath my feet, the dismal vistas followed the laws of perspective and did not dissolve and blend into the forest as I had feared they might do. Someone had told me of the little sunken chantry with the powerful echo; I found it and entered.

It was very dark; a dull light streamed through the broken tracery of the narrow windows. There were mutilated masks on the spandrels, thick toadstools grew on the stone seats of the monks and showed like stale foam on the entablatures. I tested the echo, whispering: 'Who has been worshipped here?' There came back to me like the roll of muffled drums – 'worshipped here!'

I had heard tales about what used to try to come in from the woods, and the prayers the monks put up to keep them out; a nameless altar, deep in corruption, had been discovered beneath the old wall that kept out the woods, and there was no reasonable explanation of some of the carvings in the dormitories – who was the woman with the two children seated on the waxing moon and who might be the thin morose man with the boar's head on his shoulder who lowered in his niche by the north door? I had heard tales, but I could not sort them one from another then – I was too eager to quench my curiosity while I had the opportunity. The echo pursued me as I hastened out of the chantry along the cloisters and out into the open air again.

The comfortless sky was veiled, the surly air heavy, round about me glided the dead leaves from the decayed limes supported by iron props and chains that edged the great courtyard where I found myself; the cold increased and I thought by the crackle under my feet that the ground was glazed with ice.

Three sides of me were the fronts of the monastic buildings with windows that looked into empty rooms; they had used the convent for a prison after the monks were expelled, and then for a hospital for lunatics; there were chains fastened to the walls in every cell, they said; on the fourth side of me was the church; the last of the dried and frozen refuse of the grapes was over the steps, the red imprint of the grape-crusher's feet showed on the dusty stone, the hooded steeple went up very high, I thought, into the cold vapours that were hastening up from the unseen river.

I was afraid, now that I had after exceeding toil reached my goal, that I should find the great door closed, but it yielded to the pressure of my hand and I slipped into the church.

The huge winepresses stood between the pillars and cast shadows that met in the centre of the aisle; clear glass had been put in the windows, but the visionary light seemed, with every second, to fade. Nothing remained of the holy furnishings that I remembered so well but the statues painted life-like that rested against the eastern wall; they appeared to be sainted bishops with mitres and haloes, vestments and croziers, but to look behind them was to discover the fraud – they were sawn trees and hollow with age and decay. Like the midnight music with which I was so familiar was a potent whispering in my ears – I supposed that it came from those chained lime-trees without. On the site of the altar I found him; how could I have forgotten the appointment we had? – I, who had prided myself on my constancy. This meeting had been the purpose of all my dreams; a dreadful anxiety pinched my heart that, after all, everything might go amiss.

He was stretched patiently on his tomb, sprigs of hay were scattered over his stone cloak as if they had bedded some animal by his side, the stale musty perfume of the vintage lees was in the air – or was this the scent of the dregs of the wine that had once spilled from the altar chalice?

A sense of my unutterable loneliness overwhelmed and dismayed me; I had wandered so far, I had been lost for so long; I had no hope that any anodyne would ever assuage the deadly nostalgia that tormented me. If I could have had either complete oblivion or perfect memory! But how could I endure this twilight of distorted recollections and uneasy slumbers? I was at the dead neaptide of joy.

It was the sense of eternity that was so oppressive, time seemed to hang on me like a lead weight, so that though I had arrived where I might never be again, I was too burdened to rejoice.

I touched his tomb; that was solid, the corners of the stone hurt the palms of my hands when I pressed them there; I could see the rude marks where some instrument had defaced his name – how anxious they were to conceal him from me and even from a casual, curious gaze! I picked up a handful of hay

– this had been a daisy and that a cornflower, that a blade of grass, that red-leaved sorrel.

The acorn is not yet formed that shall grow the oak that shall make the cradle to rock the wise man who shall solve my bewilderments for me.

I was aware of his loneliness impinging on my own; his utter desolation touched my sorrow like flame on a wound.

Forgotten by everyone but myself and I could not reach him; this was more than love, an essence too fine for the crucible of humanity that must escape in vapour or break the vessel that contained it; I looked at my hand laid on the tomb and was startled to see that it was, after all, the hand of a mortal woman.

The guide was calling outside the church; I heard his wheezy voice lamenting that dusk was falling and he could not clear the desolate grounds of the straggling sightseers.

I felt myself recede from his tomb as the shadows recede from the light – the sound of the human voice had cast me away from him to where I belonged.

Yet he had stirred too, raised himself to one elbow, and taken his head in his hand as if he would, at last, separate himself from his grave; but at the harsh rasp of the summoning voice he had chilled into stone again. I made a garland of the hay and wished the twisted flowerets would freshen into sap and lustre at my touch; I laid this wreath over his alabaster brows and left him; the shadows were now clustering in a thicket of fear behind the wine butts; I thought I saw nimble creatures moving there, keeping stealthily beyond my observation.

As I passed out of the church I saw the guide shambling ahead of me, shouting in a raucous voice into the swiftly falling dusk; the buildings looked sombre and rigid in the last light and an insistent wind was tugging at the chains on the drooping lime-trees.

I hastened after the guide, for I thought that some invisible menace was driving me forth, and that, for his sake, it would be better for me to go.

The guide greeted me sourly.

'You left it too late,' he said. 'You might have been locked in here for the night – and how do you think you are going to pass through the forest in the dark?'

I did not answer and he began to complain, childishly, of the things that came up out of the forest after nightfall; I smiled to think how little he knew of me.

The other visitors had gone; my carriage waited in the lee of the gate, man and horse asleep. The mist had lifted from the crystalline upper air. A heavenly star glittered in the midst of the chaplet of gilt metal constellations round the brow of the statue above the twisted ironwork.

The wood appeared so dense that it might have been solid; the trees were certainly pressing on the monastery garden walls as if they would invade and overwhelm the sacred, profaned place; one night, I thought, the trees will break through and in the morning there will be nothing but the forest, with no trace to mark where the monastery had been. Who then will find where he lies, sunk beneath so powerful an onslaught?

My driver lit his lanterns; he knew his way through the forest very well, and could, he said, find the road easily, even in the twilight hour.

It was very cold, but I would not have the hood up – the wool rug on which the dead leaves had fallen was sufficient for me; how odd to hear the old man lock the gates behind me, as if that could keep me out.

'Does he live alone in that vast, empty place?' I asked the driver.

'Not what you would call alone,' he replied, 'though there is not much human company.'

We started off briskly – the glimmering light held until we reached the forest; there were fields either side, divided from the road by old apple-trees; the fruit had long since been plucked and the boughs looked stark against the sky, which was the colour of dead lilac flowers and pellucid as running spring water.

When we reached the wood it was different; with every roll of the wheels something scuttled out of our path into the blackness under the trees; the widening spokes of light from our lantern showed me strange creatures on the lower boughs of the firs or crouching on the ground.

I thought that they pitied my loneliness and my flight, yet I knew them to be utterly unsubstantial, mere wraiths of shade.

My driver spoke over his shoulder to bid me listen to the sound of the vesper bells that floated to us from a neighbouring village, but I could not hear them. The increasing darkness pleased me; I seemed to be travelling to the very centre of loneliness where I should meet him and our different desolations would be resolved at last into a common ease.

The light of the carriage lamps fell over the front of the inn where I was staying and showed all the mottoes written in black Gothic letters over the stucco front beneath the carved gables and the wooden balconies.

I left the carriage and entered the inn; everyone was abroad; they would be, I knew, far away at some bright festival in a Christian fane where there would be scented lights, organ music, and grand singing; I thought of them with awe and dismay.

They had left a taper and candle for me in the entrance; I heard the carriage drive away into the forest as I saw the little flame spring from the hard wax; I went upstairs to my room; they had not closed the shutters and at every window I passed I saw the pine-trees, blackness on blackness with no chink to let in the starlight.

My casement was open on the forest; as I went to close it I saw him on the balcony, the garland of perished wildings still about his hard brows, his stone mantle covered the threshold of my room and he was much taller than he had looked lying on his tomb; a disc of light was between his eyes.

I knew then that this was no waking hour and the disappointment was profound, for I had resolved to put all to the test of reality.

'This is another dream,' I sighed as I turned on my hard, straight bed and felt the memorial stone above me.

'Yes,' he whispered. 'But *whose* dream? Yours or mine?'

VI

Mr Mergenthwirker's Lobblies

Nelson Bond

The same year that Orson Welles' 'The Invasion From Mars' was broadcast by CBS Radio (1938), the rival network NBC began a supernatural series destined for a long and heart-stopping run. It was called Lights Out *and it was the brainchild of a skilful radio scriptwriter named Willis Cooper who had observed the successful transfer of the comic strip character Buck Rogers from newspaper format to weekly radio adventures on NBC, and convinced the station that there was a huge public interest in tales of fantasy as a whole. The phenomenal reaction to Welles' invasion broadcast proved just how right he was! Although Cooper wrote many of the scripts for* Lights Out *himself, he occasionally used the work of other writers – and arguably his most successful adaptation was the story 'Mr Mergenthwirker's Lobblies' by Nelson Bond (1908-). Bond, a publicist by profession and rare book dealer by inclination, wrote a number of memorable novels and some excellent fantasy short stories of which this one alone would ensure his reputation. The tale of some invisible creatures who follow little Mr Mergenthwirker everywhere he goes, was discovered in the pages of* Scribner's Magazine *where it appeared in 1937 and dramatised for* Lights Out *the following year. Such was its success, that it later formed the basis for a radio series of its own as well as being adapted for the stage. (No mention of* Lights Out *would be complete without a reference to Arch Obler, the man who succeeded Willis Cooper, and wrote a tale about a chicken's heart which is stimulated by hormone injections and grows so horrifically large it eventually engulfs the world! No other medium but radio could have made such a story believable, and subsequently the broadcast has since been called 'one of the most famous single radio plays of any kind'. Perhaps not surprisingly!)*

That year instead of the raise I damn well deserved they handed me the resounding title of Assistant City Editor, which meant that in addition to my regular duties I was now responsible for the boners of the leg men. The only good break I got – if you'd call it that – was a 'private office' with my name on the door. A dingy little hole just off the City Room, littered with last year's papers, and elaborately furnished with three overflow files from the Morgue, a swivel chair with one missing caster, and a yellow oak desk neatly scalloped with cigarette scars.

The faint tap on the door gave me a chance to get my feet off the desk before I shouted; 'Come in!' The door swung open hesitantly and I saw him.

'Yes?' I said.

He stood there, blinking at me apologetically. A tiny man, hardly more than five foot one, or maybe two, with sand-coloured hair and eyes. His clothing was plain but neat. And he was nervous. His hands twitched and wriggled constantly; darting in and out of pockets, brushing imaginary pieces of lint from his lapels, fumbling at his watch chain – always on the move. He was restless on the hoof, too – shuffling and fidgeting like he had termites in his trousers.

'Are – are you the man who takes the news?' he said.

'Who, me?' I answered elaborately. 'Hell, yes! I'm the whole damned newspaper. I write the front page, lay out the ads, draw the cartoons, dig up the dirt, and sell papers on the street. Why, me and Bill Hearst – say, what do you want, anyway?'

His meek, twidgety gaze needled me. He stood there gaping as though my every word was Gospel. He jerked when I shot the question at him, and his pale eyes grew a little frightened.

'Why, I – I just wanted to tell you,' he faltered, 'that there's going to be a murder. This afternoon.'

You meet all kinds of crackpots in this racket. I grinned at him sort of cheerfully, and nodded.

'Nice going, Mr – '

'Mergenthwirker,' he supplied. 'Henry Mergenthwirker.'

'Nice going, Mr Mergenthwirker,' I said. 'You socked it right on the button that time. There *is* going to be a nice little murder this afternoon. Blood and brains all over everything. I'm just writing the headlines now. "*D.A. Slays mate in –* " '

'Oh, no!' gasped the little man. 'Not the District Attorney! Nothing like that! It's a girl up in the Bronx. A secretary named Hazel Johnson. She's going to be killed with a hammer!'

Honestly, that stopped me for a minute. He looked so darned sincere, his tiny hands fluttering around his coat lapels like bewildered moths; his tawny eyes wide and horrified. I thought: 'Perhaps this is one of those psychological cases. A potential murderer compelled to confess his crime before it happens. Perhaps it *has* happened already, and he is trying to establish an alibi.' I looked at him sharply.

'What's the gag?' I said. 'You know the girl?'

'Me?' he said. 'No, I never saw her in my life.'

'Then how do you know about the murder?'

He smiled beatifically.

'*They* told me,' he said. He gestured vaguely toward the door with one hand.

'They? Who?'

'My lobblies,' explained the little man patiently. He pointed, proudly, I thought, toward the doorway again. 'The big one's name is Japheth, but the little one is named after me. They tell me everything.'

'Now, wait a minute, buddy,' I said. 'Are you trying to tell me there's somebody in this room besides you and me?'

He rinsed his hands in a gesture of quick despair.

'Oh, *don't* tell me you can't see them!' he wailed. 'So *few* people can!' He stamped his foot in sudden exasperation. 'It's all because they *will* change colour! If they'd only stay *put*! But, no! They're forever – '

This time I got it. I rose swiftly and grabbed the little fellow by the shirt front.

'Listen, Mr Whatsis,' I told him. 'I've got things to do, but worrying about your D.T.'s isn't one of them. Now, scram! And on the way out, tell the boys in the City Room that it went over like a lead balloon.'

I pushed him, indignantly protesting, through the door, and waited until the pit-a-pat of his footsteps disappeared down the hallway. Then I strolled out into the City Room, with one eye peeled for the grins. A couple of the boys were matching nickels over by Duff Godshall's desk. I sauntered over carelessly.

'OK, boys,' I said. 'Let's have the wisecracks!'

'Tails!' said Duff. He took a nickel off the back of each of the fellows' hands; then looked at me curiously. 'Wisecracks?'

'I suppose none of you boys ever heard tell of a guy named Mergenthwirker?' I asked caustically.

Three heads shook in unison.

'It's a gag,' guessed Bill McGhee. 'Early in the day to start drinking, Len.'

'Oh, skip it!' I said wearily. 'Anyway, it didn't work, in case you're interested. Come on, who's matching who in this game?'

I had just pulled a couple of nickels from my vest pocket when the boss shoved open his door and let out a blat to high heaven.

'Hawley! Godshall! Get Maguire and light out for the Bronx. There's a hammer killing up there! A broad named Johnson!'

The funny part about it was that there was no mystery connected with this hammer job. They caught the guilty man an hour after they found the body, and he confessed right off the bat. What I mean is, there wasn't one thing to connect my nutsack visitor with the case. So the affair bothered me. I looked up the name 'Mergenthwirker' in the telephone book and the city directory, but it wasn't in either of them. I don't know just what I would have done if it *had* been. After all, you can't go to the bobbies and say, 'Look here, a guy named Mergenthwirker has two green familiars who told him there was going to be a murder.' So I puzzled over the thing for a week or so, and then it gradually dropped out of my mind. It might never have occurred to me again if I hadn't dropped into Tony's joint one night for a drink.

Tony's bar, as usual, was jammed with half-lit reformers, solving national problems in three easy lessons, so I ducked for the back room. It's a dimly lit little hole, with only about four tables. As I entered, I saw this guy Mergenthwirker sitting at the best table – the one beneath the only light – with a beer glass before him. The places on his left and right had beer glasses, too, but no one was sitting there. The sandy little man looked up as I entered.

'Oh, hello!' he said in a pleased voice. Evidently he didn't bear me any ill will for kicking him out of my office. 'Won't you join us?'

I would. I moved around to the chair on his left and started to pull it out. Mergenthwirker leaped up suddenly, slopping his beer all over the table.

'Oh, not there!' he cried. 'You'll sit on Henry!'

I took the chair across from him. Tony came out with my beer, mopped up the mess on the table, and left. The little man smiled at me apologetically.

'It's so *dark* in here,' he said. 'I guess you didn't see Henry, did you?'

'No,' I said bluntly, 'I didn't. Listen, buddy, I've been looking for you. How did you know about the Johnson murder?'

There was an astonished, half-aggrieved look in his pale eyes.

'Why, my lobblies,' he said. 'My lobblies told me.'

I jerked my head toward the empty chairs.

'Henry, here, and – '

' – and Japheth! Yes, certainly! They tell me all sorts of things. For instance' – he leaned far over the table eagerly – 'did you know the Second National was going to be robbed Tuesday?'

'The Second National?'

'Yes!' he said excitedly. 'Four men in a blue Olds will hold it up at 3:30 p.m. Only the police will catch them. They're going to smash up their car trying to escape!'

'Got all the details, haven't you?' I said.

'I *always* have all the details,' he complained. 'I had all the details before, but you' – he smiled forgivingly – 'well, it doesn't matter. Will you call Tony, please? Japheth wants more beer.'

I gulped and stared at Japheth's glass ... or maybe I stared first and then gulped. The glass was empty! And I would swear on a stack of proof sheets that I had been watching the little man every instant since I came in. And he did *not* drink that beer himself!

'Does he' – I began cautiously – 'does he drink very much beer?'

Mergenthwirker sighed.

'Barrels! Both he and Henry. But what can I do? If I don't buy it for them, they make scenes.'

'Scenes?' I repeated vaguely.

'Yes,' he confided. 'You know – pinch people on – on buses, and whisper things to girls. Especially pretty girls. *Young* girls.'

He smiled shyly, and a faint blush crept over his colourless cheeks. 'Henry's the worst. He just doesn't seem to care *what* he says to young girls. Once he even ... I mean, there was that girl in Atlantic City ... '

Tony came just then with four glasses of beer. As he renewed ours, I noted that now Henry's, as well as Japheth's, glass was empty. And this time I *knew* Mergenthwirker had not touched the beer. I paid for the round, and Tony waddled away.

'Mergenthwirker,' I said seriously, 'either you're nuts or I am. You call Japheth and Henry "lobblies". What do you mean by that?'

'Why, that's what they are, of course,' he said, his eyes round with surprise.

'But how ... or where ... did you get them?'

'I've always had them,' he said – proudly, this time. 'Ever since – oh, since I was very young. Japheth came first, but he was lonely, so after a while the little one came, too. We named him Henry, after me. Of course, he was *very* young when he came, and he had some perfectly awful habits at first. But he's starting to get over them now.'

'Habits?' I said. 'What kind of habits?'

'Oh – lobbly habits!' said Mergenthwirker airily. 'Things like pwidgeting and rikking trilks and ... eh, what's that?' He leaned to his right, listening intently, then nodded.

'Japheth says you wouldn't understand,' he told me. 'Do you mind?'

'Not at all,' I said. I was hot and cross and irritable and my watch told me it was time to grab some shuteye. 'Say, Mergenthwirker,' I said, 'I've got to run along now, but I wish you'd drop in at the office again some day soon. Bring – bring the lobblies with you.'

'Thank you, I will,' said the little man. I rose from the table, reaching for my hat.

'Oh, Japheth and Henry say thank you for the drink,' added my companion. I glanced at the table swiftly. Once more the beer glasses were empty ...

At three o'clock the next afternoon I hoked up a phony excuse to plant two of the boys and a cameraman in the Second National Bank. At 3:30 on the dot a blue Olds sedan drew up, four men stepped out, whisked briskly into the bank, covered the joint with a tommy gun, scooped up the gravy, and moved along. At 3:57 their car, closely followed by my three men and the police, clipped an elevated post on Sixth. And at 4:10 my sheet pulled the first 'beat' this burg has seen in the past six years – a complete pictorial account of the Second National robbery!

I had just finished receiving the boss's congratulations – *sans* bonus – when Mergenthwirker came in. He was beaming delightedly.

'So!' he said triumphantly.

'So!' I agreed slowly, 'you were right. I don't know how or why – but you were.'

'It's my lobblies,' Mergenthwirker boasted. 'They know everything.'

'Man,' I told him, 'with Japheth and Henry to help you, you could be the richest guy this side of Hades. Do they know the results of horse races, lotteries, football games?'

'Why – why, I suppose so,' said Mergenthwirker. 'I never stopped to think – ' His brows furrowed momentarily. 'My *goodness!* I *could*, couldn't I!'

'Looks as if,' I grunted. 'Here, won't you and the boys sit down?'

The little man was dancing with nervousness.

'Oh, *no!*' he said excitedly. 'Oh, *my!* I never even *thought* of using Henry and Japheth to – Will you come over and have a drink with us? Talk it over?'

'Why not?' I said. We went down in the elevator, Mergenthwirker jabbering six to a dozen, to the vast amusement of the elevator boy. On the street he grabbed my arm and held me back.

'Let *them* go ahead,' he whispered hoarsely. 'Perhaps they wouldn't exactly like it if they knew I was planning to – to *use* them like that. I'll have to break it sort of gently, and see what they think. I wouldn't want to – '

His words were drowned in the belligerent squawk of one of those huge, lumbering trucks that the city still allows on its main thoroughfares. The traffic light had just turned red, holding us to the curb, but a few pedestrians ahead were still scrambling, with affronted awkwardness, for the safety zone.

Mergenthwirker screamed shrilly, his tiny hands digging painfully into my arm.

'*Henry!*'

Suddenly he left me, and darted into the middle of the street with arms outthrust before him as thought to push some slighter body out of danger. A horn growled, brakes squealed viciously, somewhere a whistle shrilled, and the spattering of many voices tightened into a murmuring knot in the center of the street. Suddenly numbed with fear, I elbowed my way through the crowd. Mergenthwirker, his body grotesquely twisted, lay crumpled on the asphalt. I leaned over him and lifted his head on my arm. His eyes fluttered open, recognized me.

'Henry – ' he gasped. 'Is he all right?' His head turned stiffly, his eyes searching the press of babbling bystanders. 'Ah! There – I thought so. Then he *is* safe … ' He closed his eyes contentedly.

'Take it easy, guy,' I said. 'There'll be an ambulance here directly.'

'Ambulance!' He stared at me; his tawny eyes were wide and then they were suddenly deep with growing fear. 'For me? Oh, no – that can't be! I can't die! Japheth! Henry! What will they do without me? My lobblies – my lovely, beautiful lobblies! Nobody to talk with … nobody to buy them beer … and Henry is *so* young! What – '

'Listen,' I said, 'they'll be all right. I'll take care of them.'

There was a slow ripple through the crowd. Far down the street I heard the wailing siren of an ambulance. The little man's eyes flickered briefly, and a great weariness pressed upon their lids.

'Thank you! Thank you very much,' said Mr Mergenthwirker …

VII

Mrs Hawker's Will

Alonzo Deen Cole

The success of Mercury Theatre *and* Lights Out *in America, naturally enough prompted several other macabre anthology programmes during the decade which followed – three of which deserve to be represented in this collection:* Witch's Tales *created by Alonzo Deen Cole;* Stay Tuned For Terror *which showcased the grim humour and ghoulish imagination of Robert Bloch; and* Suspense *which had a strong inclination towards crime and detection, but also featured fantasy including some stories by the talented master of that genre Ray Bradbury. But let us take them one at a time.* Witch's Tales *was launched in New York in 1931 with a host known as 'Old Nancy the Witch' (complete with a black cat named Satan) who recounted weird, bizarre and fantastic tales. 'Grisly spectres of the restless dead arising from their tombs at midnight,' the old crone would chuckle over the air waves. 'Sorcerers brewing weird and awful potions by the light of a pale new moon. Ravening werewolves pursuing helpless prey. The horrid vampire. The murderous elemental. The mischievous poltergeist. The mournful banshee of the Irish. Magic … Satanism … Alchemy. Come – join old Nancy, the witch of Salem, and Satan, her wise black cat!' The stories which the creator of the series, Alonzo Deen Cole (1899-1959) adapted for the air were often ingenious, occasionally terrifying, and always entertaining. A prime example is 'Mrs Hawker's Will' which was broadcast in 1936, and of which 'Old Nancy' invited her listeners to 'let yer imaginations go ter work'. The invitation remains good today – just as does her echoing final comment, 'Yores for plessunt dreams!'*

The parchment shaded lamp threw an amber glow on the faces of the four people seated around the refectory table in the library of the Hawker mansion. But the light scarcely penetrated to the walls of the huge room, lined to the ceiling with tiers of books.

Barbara Turner, sitting at the foot of the table with her younger brother and aunt on either side, looked eagerly, her vivid blue eyes shining with excitement, at the man with iron grey hair opposite her.

The grey-haired man adjusted the pince-nez on his long thin nose, drew from his pocket a document, unfolded it, and smiled at Barbara.

'I shall read Mrs Hawker's will once more, Miss Turner,' he announced seriously, 'as it is vital to your interests that you conform to its terms.'

He turned back the blue paper cover of the document, smoothed it out on the table, and read:

I, Rachel Hawker, of Stalling in the County of Queens and State of New York, being of sound mind and memory, and considering the uncertainties of this transitory life, do publish and declare this to be my last WILL and TESTAMENT:

First, I order and direct that my Executor, hereinafter named, pay all my just debts and funeral expenses as soon after my decease as conveniently may be.

Second, I bequeath, in consideration of mutual esteem and affection, to Helen Turner all the property real and personal of which I die possessed, her heirs and assigns forever,

Provided that she shall live continuously and without interruption in my home at Stalling for the period of one year, and furthermore that she shall occupy the southeast bedroom which I, during my residence, occupied, for at least three hours every night between midnight and sunrise, and provided further that she shall be alone during these hours.

Third, my tomb which I have caused to be built and wherein I shall be interred is never to be removed, altered, or demolished.

Fourth, I charge and instruct my Executor to place my mortal remains in a coffin, the lid of which can be raised from the interior by means of a lever located near my right hand, and that the lid be hinged on one side and nowhere screwed or nailed down.

Fifth, I direct that my body be buried without being embalmed.

Sixth, In the event that Helen Turner for any reason whatever is unable to comply with the obligations herein mentioned, I bequeath all my property under the conditions set forth above to her next of female kin.

Seventh, I do hereby appoint and constitute F. Townsend Weeks my sole Executor of my last WILL and TESTAMENT.

'They certainly are funny conditions,' Barbara murmured thoughtfully, 'but I understand what I must do, Mr Weeks, and of course I shall do it.'

'They are curious conditions,' Mr Weeks ran his fingers through his hair and restored the paper to his pocket. 'But then, Mrs Hawker was a very curious person.'

Mrs Hawker had, in fact, been regarded by the local people as eccentric from the time when she had first built the great house fifteen years before. It seemed unaccountably strange that a woman, then sixty years of age, should require a mansion of more than twenty rooms that would have been the showplace of Stalling had she not placed it far back from the road behind a grove of towering locust trees so that it could not be seen. And during the ten years of her residence there before she died, her eccentricities heightened her reputation as a 'queer one'. Aside from an occasional charwoman who came in to clean, she employed only one servant at a time who was invariably a young woman of good breeding, and who for some reason or other rarely remained longer than six months.

Helen Turner, a trained nurse, as was her sister Barbara, had been in Mrs Hawker's employ only two weeks before the old lady's death, which proved to be a fatal day for Helen, too, as she was struck by an automobile and died before the ambulance reached the scene of the accident.

The publication of the strange will renewed the gossip about Mrs Hawker's peculiarities, and passersby tried to peer through the boxwood hedges to catch a glimpse of the marble mausoleum that she had built directly behind her home. Little was actually known about the 'queer one' except that she had spent most of her life in Tibet studying Eastern religions and that she spoke several Oriental languages. During the last ten years of her life she had never been known to leave her own residence and according to the charwoman spent nearly all her time in her bedroom which she allowed no one to enter, or in the library where Mr Weeks had just read the will.

Five years had passed since her death, during which time the will had been contested by Jeremiah Hawker, of New York. But its terms were simple and explicit and the courts had decided in favour of Barbara, the younger sister of Helen Turner.

'A very curious person, indeed,' Mr Weeks repeated.

'Well, there's one thing I'd like to ask ye,' declared Barbara's aunt, whose florid cheeks were as indicative of excitement as Barbara's shining eyes. 'Why did the auld lady leave her fortune to poor Helen, anyway, when she'd only known her for a fortnight?'

'Oh that was just another of her eccentricities, Miss Carpenter.' The lawyer smiled indulgently. 'Every time she employed a new companion she had me draw a new will.'

'I'd like to ask something too, Mr Weeks.' Rodney, Barbara's sixteen-year-old brother leaned across the table eagerly. 'What did she want that lever inside the coffin for?'

'That's an easy one. The poor lady was afraid of being buried alive, I should say. She didn't want to be embalmed either. She had all sorts of fantastic ideas, – the result of studying this Eastern occultism, I suppose.'

'Oh, yea, I see.' Rodney looked slightly bewildered.

'You've inherited quite a collection of Oriental literature, Miss Turner.' Weeks indicated with a sweep of his arm the shelves on either side of the stone fireplace. 'The books in English are on spiritism, magic, demonology, and all sorts of outlandish things. I don't know what the volumes treat of that are written in Chinese.'

'*Chinese!*' The word fairly exploded from Rodney's lips.

Barbara surveyed the bookshelves curiously. Then she said musingly, 'But, Helen implied that despite her eccentricities she was a highly intelligent old person who spent most of her time in scientific research.'

Weeks chuckled.

'Yes, I've heard that, but I don't think her studies were very scientific. You'll find some mighty queer stuff in this library. I'm afraid I must be running along.' Rising, he glanced at his watch. 'Yes, it's past eleven. I hope you'll find everything in shape.'

'Sure this is the only room we've seen so far,' remarked Miss Carpenter admiringly, 'But judging from it the whole place is sweet and clean.'

'We're all so grateful,' said Barbara fervently. 'I don't know how to thank you for all you've done.'

'Nonsense,' Weeks raised his hands deprecatingly. 'I've only acted as any honest executor would in the discharge of his duty.'

'Was it an executor's duty to meet us at the station and drive us all out here, bag and baggage?'

'That was his pleasure.' The lawyer took her hand as they reached the door. 'I've had a phone put in since you're so far from town, and I want you to telephone me if there's anything more I can do for you.'

'You've thought of everything.' Barbara slipped her arm through his as they started towards the *porte cochere* at the east side of the house. 'Oh, just see,' she exclaimed as they stepped down into the bluestone driveway. 'Aren't the grounds beautiful in the moonlight? It was dark as pitch when we drove up.'

'Mr Weeks,' Rodney asked excitedly, 'what's that little white building behind the house? Our garage?'

'No, son,' the lawyer said solemnly. 'That's Mrs Hawker's tomb.'

The small marble mausoleum gleamed white in the moonlight. Its solid bronze doors carved with the formalized design of a serpent gave it a formidable air. Then a cloud passed over the moon and the tomb faded, ghostlike into the sepulchral blackness that closed in upon them.

A shiver ran down Barbara's spine. To her it seemed that the moribund whiteness of the tomb had gleamed at them malignantly before it was swallowed by the impenetrable gloom. She heard Mr Weeks snap a switch on the dashboard of the car. Two shafts of light pierced the darkness beneath a grove of locust trees.

'It's the one thing I'm not going to like about this place, –

that tomb!' Miss Carpenter stared glumly into the darkness.

'We'll have to get used to it,' Barbara said firmly, casting off her momentary nervousness, 'since it's one of the provisions of the will.'

'Gee, but why is it so near the house?' Rodney asked huskily.

'I don't know,' Weeks admitted. 'Mrs Hawker had it built at the time she built the house. A rather gruesome idea, I always thought ... Well, good night, all; and congratulations again.'

A chorus of '*good nights*' followed the car as it started, its tyres crunching on the bluestone driveway. They watched it until it disappeared from view. The sound of the motor grew faint. From somewhere in the distance came a solitary dismal croak of a bull frog.

For a half hour after Mr Weeks' departure the three joyously explored their new home, finding treasures of Oriental art that delighted yet awed Barbara with their grotesque eeriness. It was almost midnight before she and her aunt finally left Rodney rummaging through the strange library while they went to prepare the beds for the night.

When they finished the four poster with its tester of embroidered Chinese silk, in which she was required to sleep, Barbara announced that she was going to start Rodney on his way to bed. Leaving her aunt to pick up the discarded dust-covers, she hurried downstairs and had just reached the library when the entire house was plunged into darkness. A minute later an agonized scream that seemed to pierce the solid walls filled every room of the huge mansion with a strident note of terror. Then the lights went on again.

Barbara and Rodney stood as if paralysed, white faced, staring at each other.

'What was that?' Rodney gasped.

'Rod! It was Aunt Maggie!'

The sound of her own voice startled Barbara into action. She turned and ran towards the stairs, Rodney close at her heels. He leapt past her at the foot of the stairs and started up them two at a time.

'She's in my room, – the East Room, Rod.'

'Aunt Maggie! What's wrong? Aunt Maggie!' Rodney

76 *Tune In For Fear*

shouted as he dashed ahead.

There was no answer.

They raced down the hall towards the East Room. At the doorway Rodney stopped so abruptly that Barbara crashed into him.

'Babs! Look!' The boy's voice trembled with terror.

On the bed lay Miss Carpenter, one hand clutched convulsively about her throat, the other dangling, limp. From her chalk-white face, distorted with an unhuman grimace, her lifeless dilated eyes stared at them as if they still beheld something insupportably horrible, – eyes glassy yet lustreless, ghastly, petrified with a perpetual expression of horror.

Barbara steadied her nerves, then stepped resolutely forward. She glanced around the room. Rodney still stood hesitant in the doorway. Nothing had been disturbed. The room was just as she had left it. There was no sign of a struggle.

Barbara felt dizzy, sick. To death she had long become accustomed, as does any nurse, but here was something more horrible than death; something unexplainable, demoniacal. She clenched her fists in an effort to control her emotion.

'She's dead, Rod,' she said, huskily. 'Phone the police to come quickly.'

She sank on her knees beside the bed, sobbing, burying her face in a pillow.

An hour later Dr Randall, the police surgeon, had completed his preliminary examination. He glanced sympathetically at Barbara and turned with an official air toward Lieutenant Crane, the officer in charge of the investigation.

'You still insist, Doc,' the lieutenant asked sceptically, 'that this woman was *frightened* to death?'

'I do,' the doctor replied firmly. 'Until an autopsy shows me some organic weakness that isn't apparent now, I'll say she died of paralysis of the heart muscles brought about by sudden shock – and the expression of her face and eyes indicate that shock was caused by sheer stark terror.'

'But what could have frightened her?' A sob escaped as Barbara tried to speak. 'There was nothing here to do it.'

'You two entered this room almost immediately after she screamed?' The officer looked from Barbara to Rodney.

'Yeah.' Rodney's voice was shaky. 'An' the room was just like you see it now.'

The lieutenant's gaze swept the room and came to rest on Sergeant Michael Ryan, a tall, ruddy-faced young man with flaming hair.

'You see, Ryan, she couldn't have been frightened by anything she saw through those windows. The shutters are closed and the shades drawn.'

Ryan's sinewy fingers stroked his rather prominent jaw. He seemed hesitant to answer. Finally he drawled, 'Yes, sir,' stared meditatively at the ceiling and continued. 'I've checked every door and window in this house. They're all bolted on the inside. And I've searched in every nook and cranny. There's nobody in the place besides ourselves.'

'There you are, Miss.' The lieutenant turned to Barbara. 'The doctor's explanation is the only one possible, and since she died of fright she must have, under the circumstances, been scared by her own imagination.'

'That's impossible!' Barbara insisted. 'She wasn't that kind! Besides, someone must have turned out those lights.'

'And turned 'em on again,' Rod added.

'That was probably caused by defective wiring. I'll have the electric company check up on it.' The lieutenant smiled tolerantly. 'And now, Miss, since this is a medical case, not a police matter, we'll be going.'

'Look, Lieutenant,' Ryan said with slow deliberation, 'do you mind puttin' me on duty here for a few days?'

'What for? The case is closed.'

'I've kinda got a notion it's not.'

'What do you mean?' the lieutenant snapped.

'Well, sir … ' The sergeant paused irritatingly.

Suddenly the lieutenant laughed.

'I know, you think a *ghost* did the frightening!' He turned to Barbara. 'The sergeant's quite an authority on spooks. He probably thinks the house is haunted.'

'I'm not suspecting any ghost of bein' in here tonight, sir,' Ryan said calmly, 'for I've just seen something that no ghost could leave behind.'

Ryan crossed the room and took from the back of a chair two long white hairs that had been snagged by a button of the slip cover. He drew them slowly between his index finger and thumb. Then he looked at Crane with keenly serious eyes.

'These are human hairs,' he announced.

'What of it?' the lieutenant scoffed. 'They may have been there for days – or years, for that matter.'

'Maybe so, sir,' Ryan shrugged his shoulders, 'but I don't think so. They're a little too unusual. I'm six feet tall myself and these hairs are almost as long as I am.'

During the following two days and nights Sergeant Ryan did not leave the house except for a brief inspection of Mrs Hawker's tomb, whose bronze doors he found sealed. They obviously had not been opened in years. After examining every part of the building for possible clues, he concentrated his attention upon the library. There, on the day after the death of Miss Carpenter, Barbara found him reading one of the Chinese volumes and expressed her astonishment.

'Oh,' he explained, smiling broadly, 'my mother was Irish, my father a Scots sea-captain, and I was born in the harbour of Hong Kong.'

'And learned to say *ma-ma* in Chinese, I suppose,' Barbara teased. His presence in the house had done much to mitigate the unhappiness of the last two days, both for her and Rod.

'Well, the Irish were always good at languages,' he drawled.

'I'm Scotch-Irish, too.'

'You are?' Ryan's blue eyes fairly danced. 'You know, the first minute I looked at you I said to myself, now there's too nice a girl to be anything but Scotch-Irish.'

Barbara laughed, but the colour in her cheeks heightened. She changed the subject abruptly.

'Do you really believe in ghosts?'

'Not literally, but I sort of keep an open mind about things of that kind.' Ryan restored the book to its place on the shelf. 'When I was in China I learned a lot about Eastern philosophy. Most folks are apt to say that certain things can't be just because those things have never been part of their personal experience. I've made sort of a hobby of what you might call the supernatural, – the boys kid me about the funny books I read. Well, sometimes things *do* happen that you can't explain away just by saying they could not.'

'And do you think these books will throw some light on poor Aunt Maggie's death?'

A sudden surprised look came into Ryan's eyes.

'It's funny you happened to say *throw light on*. It fitted rather neatly into my thoughts.'

'I don't understand.' Barbara seated herself on the large chair by the table and looked at him seriously.

'You see, in every language and every religion, the word *light* is associated with truth, and *darkness* with evil. We speak of the *Prince of Darkness* and of *dark forces*. And the sun that preserves life destroys the dead.'

After a moment or two of reflection Barbara asked, 'Is that why you insist on my burning that smelly oil lamp in my room at night?'

'The lights went out night before last,' the sergeant answered quickly. 'They might go out again. I don't want you frightened. When I've finished examining the wiring, we'll remove the oil lamp, Miss Turner.'

Barbara detected evasiveness in Ryan's answer. She had thought it strange that he should have sent Rodney into town to buy a kerosene lamp – of all things – and that he should insist upon her sleeping with the bedroom door ajar. Twice during the night she had awakened and looking out had seen the detective in an arm chair that he had placed close to the door.

Later in the day her bewilderment increased. She had gone to the library to speak to Sergeant Ryan and found the room empty. On the table lay a pad of paper and beside it a fountain pen. Barbara received a shock when she saw the heading above the methodically written notes on the top sheet:

Notes on Carpenter Murder.

The sergeant was convinced that her aunt had been murdered! Her eyes hurried down the page:

1. Body on back. Was probably standing by bed, facing east, – otherwise, face down.

2. Vision from that position practically all of room.

3. Hairs found at opposite end of room from bed, i.e. beyond the door to hall.

4. Re impenetrability of light zone. *Phenomena of Psychic*

Vibrations, vol. IX, p. 246 ff. Transmigration, reincarnation, see *The Mastery of the Great Lama*, vol. I. Hypnosis and Vital suspension. Protraction.

5. Wiring OK. Trace trunk line in basement.
6. Trunk line disappears in solid concrete.
7. Hairs, 5 ft 8 ins less 3 ft ? ins equals 2 ft ? ins 2 ft ? ins ÷ 5 equals about 6 ins 6 ins a year.

As Barbara finished the last cryptic note she smiled. The sergeant's theories, whatever they might be, were fantastic. She liked Ryan, she suddenly realized, liked his lithe panther-like stride, his slow speech. A strange combination, she reflected, – this long limbed man who was alternately serious almost to the point of solemnness and then laughing or joking in way that made the corners of his eyes crinkle.

But at that moment Sergeant Ryan was neither solemn nor laughing, and could she have seen him she might have agreed with the men at headquarters that he was 'nuts'. For having gone over every inch of the furniture in Barbara's bedroom for the third time, having rolled up the silk Chinese rug and crawled about on hands and knees, pounding the floor with his fists, he was now sitting in a chair intently preoccupied in the unravelling of long strands of cream-coloured yarn. The five piles separated, he began to untwist and knot together the flimsy strands that composed them. Finally he got to his feet and beginning at the left side of the room, slowly progressed around it, hammering brads, so tiny that they were practically invisible, into the pine panelling of the walls. Then he tied the gossamer thread he had spun from the yarn around the first brad, twisted it tightly drawn around the second, and so on, following his previous route around the room, zigzagging up and down the walls until they were covered with a web that for invisibility and symmetry might well have been envied by a spider. Having surveyed his handiwork with evident satisfaction, he strode rapidly down the hall on his way to the library.

'I was looking for you,' Barbara announced as he entered the room.

'That's music to my ears.' The sergeant smiled. 'From now

on I'll see that you don't have to. I shan't let you out of my sight ... Barb – Miss Turner,' he added earnestly, 'I want to try an experiment tonight, – a dangerous one. Have you confidence in me?'

'Of course.' Barbara looked into his large serious eyes.

'You won't be afraid?' He took her hands in his.

'Not if you'll be there, too.'

Sergeant Ryan was suddenly aware of the fragrance of her soft brown hair. His clasp tightened, then abruptly relaxed.

'Tonight you must turn out the oil lamp, – at midnight.'

Sergeant Ryan and Rodney had been sitting in the hall on either side of the open door to Barbara's room for more than an hour. All the lights in the great house had, with a single exception, been turned off. From far down the hallway came a faint glimmer which barely penetrated to them, and seemed to increase by contrast the darkness. In some distant room a clock chimed one doleful, reverberating note.

Ryan looked at the luminous dial of his watch.

'One-thirty,' he whispered.

'Uh huh.'

He heard Rodney stir sleepily in his chair.

'Are you all right, Barbara?' His whisper was louder.

No answer.

'She musta gone to sleep.' Rodney's whisper came through the darkness. 'An' you told her she had to stay awake.'

'Poor kid, must be worn out after the strain of these two days.'

The sergeant's fingers caressed the cool barrel of the Colt automatic in his side pocket. From his hip he took a flashlight and laid it on his lap. Then he settled back in the chair, his gaze fixed on the light, listening intently, straining to catch the slightest sound.

A half hour of deadly monotony passed. He heard Rodney's rhythmic breathing. The light glowed steadily, hypnotically. He shifted his position. The light blinked once and then went out.

Cautiously Ryan reached for Rodney's shoulder and felt the answering pressure of the boy's hand.

'On guard?' he breathed.

Somewhere a board creaked. The sound seemed to come from down the hall. Then silence. The blood pulsed at Ryan's temples like tiny blows of a hammer. He leaned forward, his muscles tensed, in an agony of alertness.

'Help!'

A single scream of terror screeched through the darkness.

Ryan bounded through the doorway.

Something swished past him with the speed of a bat, fanning foul air against his face. He flashed on the light. The sight before him turned his stomach. An animated corpse glared at him from phosphorescent eyesockets. Its face covered with dried hard skin, coffee coloured, was half concealed by the long straggly hair, white, blotched with yellow, that hung about the mummified body.

Fire spat from Ryan's gun. A little spurt, chalkly white, shot from the creature's body. Its lipless mouth grinning, it backed away. He fired five more bullets through the cadaver.

'Oh God!' he heard Barbara scream behind him, and whirled around. He saw her cover her face with her hands as Rodney put his arm protectively about her.

Then he spun back, his arm raised to hurl the empty revolver at the hideous monster.

The hairy thing had vanished.

Barbara, reassured by Ryan's finding that the lights could be switched on again, soon had her nerves under control.

'Sorry I went to pieces that way,' she said in answer to his solicitous questions. 'It's not what you'd expect of a trained nurse, is it? But to wake up to find it standing by my bed, its hands over my mouth! It wasn't human, – it smelled of mould and earth and death! It tried to smother me while I slept!'

'Thank the good Lord you're all right!' Ryan said solemnly. 'I'd never forgive myself if ... '

'But where did it go?' Rodney interrupted.

'We'll soon find out.'

The sergeant went to the other end of the room and began examining the wall. Rodney and Barbara watched with intense excitement.

'Here we are!' Ryan announced shortly. 'The strands of yarn are broken from here to the floor.' He pointed to the seam of the panelling a foot above his head.

Taking a gimlet from his pocket he screwed it well into the pine and then pulled. A section of the wall swung into the room. It had been backed with a solid oak planking four inches thick.

'Sure the old buzzard didn't miss a trick!' There was a note of admiration in his voice. 'She had those heavy planks screwed to the back of the panel so you couldn't tell it was hollow by tapping the wall ... Hello!' He bent to the floor and picked up an oval strip of hard yellow substance about five inches long.

'What is it?' Rodney was peering at it over his shoulder. 'It looks like a claw.'

'It is, of a sort,' the sergeant murmured, half to himself. 'It's a finger nail and I've kinda got a notion it proves my theory. They grow about an inch a year.'

'What do you mean?' Barbara asked in bewilderment. 'Did it belong to that – that creature, or whatever it was?'

'This is Mrs Hawker's finger nail. She was the creature we saw.'

'But she's dead!' The words came from Barbara and Rodney almost simultaneously.

'Do you mean her ghost?' Barbara added hesitantly.

'No, ghosts don't leave hair behind, nor finger nails. She may be legally dead, and technically too, since there's a suspension of animation. What I think is that she's in a condition of self-hypnosis that arrests all organic functions. There was a lot about it in those books of hers. Her will remains dominant so that she can partially reanimate herself for intervals. I kinda had a notion of what she was after when I heard the terms of her will.'

'But what *is* she after?' Barbara demanded.

'I'll explain later. I've a little job that has to be done right away. You wait here, Rod, with your sister until I come back.'

Sergeant Ryan stepped through the space made by the open panel. His flash-light revealed narrow precipitous stairs descending to the right. Slowly he went down them, counting twenty four steps. He judged then that he had reached the level of the floor below. The stairs made a right angle to the west, presumably passing within the outside wall of the house.

Twenty more steps he descended. Here the air smelled of damp earth. The passage described a semicircle and continued due east. He paced two hundred feet between the wet walls that sparkled before the flash-light. Then the passage abruptly ended.

Ryan swung the light in an arc. Directly above his head was a trapdoor. He pushed with his left hand. It resisted his pressure. Crouched on his knees he slipped the flash-light into his hip pocket and pushed with both hands. The trapdoor swung upwards as he gradually rose to a standing position. The air was suffocatingly foul.

Suddenly from behind him hard fingers that had the strength of steel closed about his throat, jerking him backwards so that his neck was forced against the edge of the floor above. He drove his fist upward into the darkness; futilely thrashed the air. His lungs seemed on fire. Bright specks whirled before his eyes. Slowly his muscles relaxed. His body fell limply to the floor of the passage.

'Mr Ryan! Mr Ryan!'

The voice seemed to come from a great distance. Then it was nearer, louder.

'Sergeant Ryan!'

His eyes blinked open. He saw Barbara bending over him, and Rodney, a flash-light in his hand, crouching by her side.

'Thank heaven,' Barbara murmured, tears filling her eyes. 'We thought that ghastly thing had killed you.'

'Not quite.' Ryan sat up, rubbing his neck and smiled feebly. 'It's worth being half killed to know you'd be sorry.'

'Are you badly hurt?'

'Now that I've got my breath back again there's nothing wrong with me at all. But what are you two doing here?'

'I – we couldn't let you go down those steps alone to meet the hideous monster. Rod got his flash-light and we followed. When we turned the corner back there we could see you standing up – that is, all of you but your head and shoulders. Then suddenly as we came close you fell to the ground.'

'You probably saved my life, Miss Turner,' Ryan declared. 'The thing had a strangle hold on me, but it let go when you came with the light. They're always afraid of light ... You're a mighty brave young lady, and I owe my life to you.'

Thrusting the flash-light ahead of him through the trapdoor he got to his feet. 'Excuse me a minute.'

As he raised his body through the opening he saw the lid of the coffin slowly close. With a single bound he reached the side of the coffin and began screwing the gimlet through the edge of the lid, pinning it fast.

Shortly before twelve the following night Ryan was addressing those gathered about the refectory table in the library. Barbara, her blue eyes intent upon the sergeant's face, sat beside Rodney. Opposite them were Mr Weeks and Lieutenant Crane.

'I have a notion Mrs Hawker probably learned much of this,' he was saying, 'during the years she lived in Tibet. She continued her studies and perfected the art here in this house. I finally found the books which gave the rigmarole about the suspension of life through self-hypnosis. She knew she would be able to remain in what the Tibetians call the state of *necrocoma* for an indefinite period. She'd also learned the art of metemsychosis.'

'And what the devil is that?' Crane's attitude was half bantering half respectful.

'Well, it's the transmigration of the soul and mind into another body. Mrs Hawker was an old woman. She wanted to reincarnate her mind and spirit in the body of a young and beautiful girl.' His eyes rested involuntarily on Barbara before he continued: 'So of course the will is understandable with its "next of female kin" and injunction against embalming.'

'But why the "three hours between midnight and dawn"? Couldn't she get her victim any time?' Weeks asked.

'No, so far as I can find out transmigration can only be accomplished during those hours, and besides there's the matter of light. Any light is revolting to a body in a necrocomatose trance, and the ultra violet ray or sunlight is fatal if the body is in a semi-animated condition. That's why she had the electric switch installed, so she can turn off all the lights in the house at once.'

'You haven't located the switch yet, sergeant?' asked the lieutenant.

'No sir. The wire goes into the solid concrete of the foundation. It must have been done when the house was built.'

'A most amazing case!' Mr Weeks removed his pince-nez nervously. 'How do you propose to proceed, sergeant?'

'Everything is already prepared. I've forced the bronze doors of the vault and have installed inside it electric lamps that will throw ultra violet rays all about the coffin at the proper time. That cable you saw running out through the window to the East end of the house carries the current.'

'Wouldn't it be simpler to open the coffin during the day and expose it to the sunlight?' Crane asked.

'No sir. It's only when Mrs Hawker's evil spirit voluntarily lifts her hypnotic trance that it can be completely destroyed, – as we've seen, between midnight and dawn.' He glanced at his watch and then at the lieutenant. 'It's time for us to go to the tomb now, sir.'

Sergeant Ryan finally gave in to the entreaties of Barbara and Rodney to be allowed to accompany the three men.

'If there's any danger I ought to be there,' she insisted. 'After all I am a trained nurse.'

'Sure there'll be no danger. The flood lights will do their work mighty quick.'

'Then if there's no danger, why can't we come with you?'

Before this irrefutable logic and Barbara's large pleading eyes, the sergeant submitted. He was firm in his decision that she and Rod must stay with Mr Weeks outside the great bronze doors while he and Crane took their positions inside the vault.

The night was cloudy, much to Ryan's satisfaction, but the faint light from a few stars made the ghostly figures of the watchers partially discernible.

'Wait till the lid's wide open,' Ryan whispered to Crane, 'before you switch on the lights.' He had tested them a moment before, and found their brilliance almost blinding.

For a half hour, an hour, the vigil lasted. Then there came the sound of scraping inside the coffin. The lid began to inch upwards, noiselessly. Ryan waited, tense. It reached a vertical position and stopped. Two luminous eyesockets shone in the darkness.

'Lights!' Ryan yelled.

The mausoleum remained in darkness.

'Lights, turn on the lights!' he repeated, urgently.

Crane's voice, almost hysterical, answered.

'They won't work. Something's wrong!'

'For God's sake, hurry!'

The air had suddenly become foul. Dimly they saw the long haired monster swing over the side of the coffin, crouch and spring at Ryan's throat. His knuckles cracked against bone. Long skeleton fingers shut off his wind, knife-like nails bit into his throat.

Crane rushed at the struggling figures. His foot struck the edge of the trapdoor, and he was hurled against the opposite wall.

'The flash light, Rod!' Barbara screamed.

Rodney sent a shaft of light into the tomb, revealing Ryan, purple-faced, hammering his fists against the cadaver's skull.

Barbara darted forward.

'Don't go in there!' Weeks shouted, catching her by the shoulder. 'The creature's deadly!'

'It's killing Mr Ryan,' she half sobbed, half screamed. 'Let me go!'

With a quick jerk she freed herself and dashed into the vault to the open coffin. Frantically she felt about its interior.

Suddenly there was blinding light.

The bony hands fell away from Ryan's throat. He staggered back, gasping air into his lungs.

For a moment Mrs Hawker's corpse stood rigid. The leathery skin of her face turned darker brown, then black. Fingernails clattered from her hands to the floor. The long yellow-stained hair writhed, coiled like snakes, and fell in an ugly mass at her feet. Then the whole cadaver collapsed. In horror they watched it disintegrate, become a pool of putrescence, and vanish.

At Barbara's sob Ryan, his face scratched and bleeding from the creature's nails, went to her.

'It's destroyed now forever. You've saved my life again, Barb – Miss Turner.' His voice was shaky but his eyes, looking deeply into hers, showed unconcealed admiration. 'But how did you ever guess the switch was in the coffin?'

Struggling to control her nerves, Barbara smiled tremulously.

'I thought she was killing you,' she said, unashamed of her

tears. Then in answer to his question, 'It *had* to be there or she couldn't have switched off the current ... I just kinda had a notion.'

VIII

The Bat Is My Brother

Robert Bloch

The series Stay Tuned For Terror *which was launched in 1945 was the idea of Robert Bloch (1917-), then one of the leading contributors to the famous pulp magazine,* Weird Tales, *and destined in 1959 to become world-famous as the author of Alfred Hitchcock's best-known film,* Psycho. *Bloch himself explained in the pages of* Weird Tales *how the chance to realise a radio dream came true. 'For many years,' he said, 'I've had certain pet ideas about doing a radio "horror show" of my own in which the emphasis would be placed on atmosphere; featuring a dramatic narrator and original musical scores running through the programme. I confess to being irritated, at times, by the type of scream-opera usually offered to listeners. But now opportunity has knocked on the lid of my coffin in the shape of an assignment to adapt my own stories for* Stay Tuned For Terror *the majority of which will come from the pages of* Weird Tales.' *The association with the magazine undoubtedly helped generate interest in the series which was also well-served by an astute producer, Johnnie Neblett, and the gravel-voiced narrator, Craig Dennis. It also got off to a memorable start with an adaption of one of Bloch's most popular stories from* Weird Tales, 'The Bat Is My Brother', *for which the author wrote the following introduction: 'I recently asked myself, "What would you do if you were a vampire?" The only answer I could think of was, "Go out and get a bite to eat." So I sat down and began to consider the question. What are a vampire's personal problems? How does he adapt himself to his peculiar limitations? How far is his nocturnal existence allied to that of the swing-shift worker? How does a vampire regard his own condition? Why is it that vampires, in weird fiction, are invariably lone operators? If vampirism is transmissible, why don't the ranks of the*

89

Undead increase in mathematical progression? With centuries to live, why aren't vampires omniscient, or at least wise enough to organise and plan domination? You won't find the answers to these questions in Dracula. *I don't know if all of them are in "The Bat Is My Brother". But I've tried to deal with these interesting little matters in my usual style, and I hope listeners (including the vampires amongst them, of course) will get a few ideas. I am always glad to give a vampire something he can get his teeth into. Hoping you are the same — Robert Bloch.'*

I

It began in twilight – a twilight I could not see.

My eyes opened on darkness, and for a moment I wondered if I were still asleep and dreaming. Then I slid my hands down and felt the cheap lining of the casket, and I knew that this nightmare was real.

I wanted to scream, but who can hear screams through six feet of earth above a grave?

Better to save my breath and try to save my sanity. I fell back, and the darkness rose all around me. The darkness, the cold, clammy darkness of death.

I could not remember how I had come here, or what hideous error had brought about my premature interment. All I knew was that I lived – but unless I managed to escape, I would soon be in a condition horribly appropriate to my surroundings.

Then began that which I dare not remember in detail. The splintering of wood, the burrowing struggle through loosely-packed grave earth; the gasping hysteria accompanying my clawing, suffocated progress to the sane surface of the world above.

It is enough that I finally emerged. I can only thank poverty for my deliverance – the poverty which had placed me in a flimsy, unsealed coffin and a pauper's shallow grave.

Clotted with sticky clay, drenched with cold perspiration, racked by utter revulsion, I crawled forth from betwixt the gaping jaws of death.

Dusk crept between the tombstones, and somewhere to my left the moon leered down to watch the shadowy legions that conquered in the name of Night.

The moon saw me, and a wind whispered furtively to brooding trees, and the trees bent low to mumble a message to all those sleeping below their shade.

I grew restless beneath the moon's glaring eye, and I wanted to leave this spot before the trees had told my secret to the nameless, numberless dead.

Despite my desire, several minutes passed before I summoned strength to stand erect, without trembling.

Then I breathed deeply of fog and faint putridity; breathed, and turned away along the path.

It was at that moment the figure appeared.

It glided like a shadow from the deeper shadows haunting the trees, and as the moonlight fell upon a human face I felt my heart surge in exultation.

I raced towards the waiting figure, words choking in my throat as they fought for prior utterance.

'You'll help me, won't you?' I babbled. 'You can see … they buried me down there … I was trapped … alive in the grave … out now … you'll understand … I can't remember how it began, but … you'll help me?'

A head moved in silent assent.

I halted, regaining composure, striving for coherency.

'This is awkward,' I said, more quietly. 'I've really no right to ask you for assistance. I don't even know who you are.'

The voice from the shadows was only a whisper, but each word thundered in my brain.

'I am a vampire,' said the stranger.

Madness. I turned to flee, but the voice pursued me.

'Yes, I am a vampire,' he said. 'And … *so are you!*'

II

I must have fainted, then. I must have fainted, and he must have carried me out of the cemetery, for when I opened my eyes once more I lay on a sofa in his house.

The panelled walls loomed high, and shadows crawled across the ceiling beyond the candlelight. I sat up, blinked, and stared at the stranger who bent over me.

I could see him now, and I wondered. He was of medium

height, grey-haired, clean-shaven, and clad discreetly in a dark business suit. At first glance he appeared normal enough.

As his face glided towards me, I stared closer, trying to pierce the veil of his seeming sanity, striving to see the madness beneath the prosaic exterior of dress and flesh.

I stared and saw that which was worse than any madness.

At close glance his countenance was cruelly illumined by the light. I saw the waxen pallor of his skin, and what was worse than that, the peculiar corrugation. For his entire face and throat was covered by a web of tiny wrinkles, and when he smiled it was with a mummy's grin.

Yes, his face was white and wrinkled; white, wrinkled, and long dead. Only his lips and eyes were alive, and they were red ... *too* red. A face as white as corpse-flesh, holding lips and eyes as red as blood.

He smelled *musty*.

All these impressions came to me before he spoke. His voice was like the rustle of the wind through a mortuary wreath.

'You are awake? It is well.'

'Where am I? And who are you?' I asked the questions but dreaded an answer. The answer came.

'You are in my house. You will be safe here, I think. As for me, I am your guardian.'

'Guardian?'

He smiled. I saw his teeth. Such teeth I had never seen, save in the maw of a carnivorous beast. And yet – wasn't *that* the answer?

'You are bewildered, my friend. Understandably so. And that is why you need a guardian. Until you learn the ways of your new life, I shall protect you.' He nodded. 'Yes, Graham Keene, I shall protect you.'

'Graham Keene.'

It was my name. I knew it *now*. But how did *he* know it?

'In the name of mercy,' I groaned, 'tell me what has happened to me!'

He patted my shoulder. Even through the cloth I could feel the icy weight of his pallid fingers. They crawled across my neck like worms, like wriggling white worms –

'You must be calm,' he told me. 'This is a great shock, I know. Your confusion is understandable. If you will just relax a bit and listen, I think I can explain everything.'

I listened.

'To begin with, you must accept certain obvious facts. The first being – that you are a vampire.'

'But – '

He pursed his lips, his *too* red lips, and nodded.

'There is no doubt about it, unfortunately. Can you tell me how you happened to be emerging from a grave?'

'No. I don't remember. I must have suffered a cataleptic seizure. The shock gave me partial amnesia. But it will come back to me. I'm all right, I must be.'

The words rang hollowly even as they gushed from my throat.

'Perhaps. But I think not.' He sighed and pointed.

'I can prove your condition to you easily enough. Would you be so good as to tell me what you see behind you, Graham Keene?'

'Behind me?'

'Yes, on the wall.'

I stared.

'I don't see anything.'

'Exactly.'

'But – '

'*Where is your shadow?*'

I looked again. There was no shadow, no silhouette. For a moment my sanity wavered. Then I stared at him. 'You have no shadow either,' I exclaimed, triumphantly. 'What does that prove?'

'That I am a vampire,' he said, easily. 'And so are you.'

'Nonsense. It's just a trick of the light,' I scoffed.

'Still sceptical? Then explain this optical illusion.' A bony hand proffered a shining object.

I took it, held it. It was a simple pocket mirror.

'Look.'

I looked.

The mirror dropped from my fingers and splintered on the floor.

'There's no reflection!' I murmured.

'Vampires have no reflections.' His voice was soft. He might have been reasoning with a child.

'If you still doubt,' he persisted, 'I advise you to feel your pulse. Try to detect a heartbeat.'

Have you ever listened for the faint voice of hope to sound within you ... knowing that it alone can save you? Have you ever listened and heard nothing? Nothing but the silence of *death?*

I knew it then, past all doubt. I was of the Undead ... the Undead who cast no shadows, whose images do not reflect in mirrors, whose hearts are forever stilled, but whose bodies live on – live, and walk abroad, and take nourishment.

Nourishment!

I thought of my companion's red lips and his pointed teeth. I thought of the light blazing in his eyes. A light of hunger. Hunger for what?

How soon must I share that hunger?

He must have sensed the question, for he began to speak once more.

'You are satisfied that I speak the truth, I see. That is well. You must accept your condition and then prepare to make the necessary adjustments. For there is much you have to learn in order to face the centuries to come.

'To begin with, I will tell you that many of the common superstitions about – people like us – are false.'

He might have been discussing the weather, for all the emotion his face betrayed. But I could not restrain a shudder of revulsion at his words.

'They say we cannot abide garlic. That is a lie. They say we cannot cross running water. Another lie. They say that we must lie by day in the earth of our own graves. That's picturesque nonsense.

'These things, and these alone, are true. Remember them, for they are important to your future. We must sleep by day and rise only at sunset. At dawn an overpowering lethargy bedrugs our senses, and we fall into a coma until dusk. We need not sleep in coffins – that is sheer melodrama, I assure you! – but it is best to sleep in darkness, and away from any chance of discovery by men.

'I do not know why this is so, any more than I can account for other phenomena relative to the disease. For vampirism is a disease, you know.'

He smiled when he said it. I didn't smile. I groaned.

'Yes, it is a disease. Contagious, of course, and transmissible in the classic manner, through a bite. Like rabies. What reanimates the body after death no one can say. And why it is necessary to take certain forms of nourishment to sustain existence, I do not know. The daylight coma is a more easily classified medical phenomenon. Perhaps an allergy to the direct actinic rays of the sun.

'I am interested in these matters, and I have studied them.

'In the centuries to come I shall endeavour to do some intensive research on the problem. It will prove valuable in perpetuating my existence, and yours.'

The voice was harsher now. The slim fingers clawed the air in excitement.

'Think of that, for a moment, Graham Keene,' he whispered. 'Forget your morbid superstitious dread of this condition and look at the reality.

'Picture yourself as you were before you awoke at sunset. Suppose you had remained there, inside that coffin, nevermore to awaken! Dead – dead for all eternity!'

He shook his head. 'You can thank your condition for an escape. It gives you a new life, not just for a few paltry years, but for centuries. Perhaps – forever!

'Yes, think and give thanks! You need never die, now. Weapons cannot harm you, nor disease, nor the workings of age. You are immortal – and I shall show you how to live like a god!'

He sobered. 'But that can wait. First we must attend to our needs. I want you to listen carefully now. Put aside your silly prejudices and hear me out. I will tell you that which needs be told regarding our nourishment.

'It isn't easy, you know.

'There aren't any schools you can attend to learn what to do. There are no correspondence courses or books of helpful information. You must learn everything through your own efforts. Everything.

'Even so simple and vital a matter as biting the neck – using the incisors properly – is entirely a matter of personal judgment.

'Take that little detail, just as an example. You must choose the classic trinity to begin with – the time, the place, and the girl.

'When you are ready, you must pretend that you are about to kiss her. Both hands go under her ears. That is important, to hold her neck steady, and at the proper angle.

'You must keep smiling all the while, without allowing a betrayal of intent to creep into your features or your eyes. Then you bend your head. You kiss her throat. If she relaxes, you turn your mouth to the base of her neck, open it swiftly and place the incisors in position.

'Simultaneously – it *must* be simultaneously – you bring your left hand up to cover her mouth. The right hand must find, seize, and pinion her hands behind her back. No need to hold her throat now. The teeth are doing that. Then, and only then, will instinct come to your aid. It must come then, because once you begin, all else is swept away in the red, swirling blur of fulfillment.'

I cannot describe his intonation as he spoke, or the unconscious pantomime which accompanied the incredible instructions. But it is simple to name the look that came into his eyes.

Hunger.

'Come, Graham Keene,' he whispered. 'We must go now.'

'Go? Where?'

'To dine,' he told me. 'To dine!'

III

He led me from the house, and down a garden pathway through a hedge.

The moon was high, and as we walked along a windswept bluff, flying figures spun a moving web across the moon's bright face.

My companion shrugged.

'Bats,' he said. And smiled.

'They say that – we – have the power of changing shape. That we become bats,or wolves. Alas, it's only another superstition. Would that it were true! For then our life would be easy. As it is, the search for sustenance in mortal form is hard. But you will soon understand.'

I drew back. His hand rested on my shoulder in cold command.

'Where are you taking me?' I asked.

'To food.'

Irresolution left me. I emerged from nightmare, shook myself into sanity.

'No – I won't!' I murmured. 'I can't – '

'You must,' he told me. 'Do you want to go back to the grave?'

'I'd rather,' I whispered. 'Yes, I'd rather die.'

His teeth gleamed in the moonlight.

'That's the pity of it,' he said. 'You can't die. You'll weaken without sustenance, yes. And you will appear to be dead. Then, whoever finds you will put you in the grave.

'But you'll be alive down there. How would you like to lie there undying in the darkness ... writhing as you decay ... suffering the torments of red hunger as you suffer the pangs of dissolution?

'How long do you think that goes on? How long before the brain itself is rotted away? How long must one endure the charnal consciousness of the devouring worm? Does the very dust still billow in agony?'

His voice held horror.

'That is the fate you escaped. But it is still the fate that awaits you unless you dine with me.

'Besides, it isn't something to avoid, believe me. And I am sure, my friend, that you already feel the pangs of – appetite.'

I could not, dared not answer.

For it was true. Even as he spoke, I felt hunger. A hunger greater than any I had ever known. Call it a cringe, call it a desire – call it lust. I felt it gnawing deep within me. Repugnance was nibbled away by the terrible teeth of growing need.

'Follow me,' he said, and I followed. Followed along the bluff and down a lonely country road.

We halted abruptly on the highway. A blazing neon sign winked incongruously ahead.

I read the absurd legend.

'DANNY'S DRIVE-IN.'

Even as I watched, the sign blinked out.

'Right,' whispered my guardian. 'It's closing time. They will be leaving now.'

'Who?'

'Mr Danny and his waitress. She serves customers in their cars. They always leave together, I know. They are locking up for the night now. Come along and do as you are told.'

I followed him down the road. His feet crunched gravel as he stalked towards the now darkened drive-in stand. My stride quickened in excitement. I moved forward as though pushed by a gigantic hand. The hand of hunger –

He reached the side door of the shack. His fingers rasped the screen.

An irritable voice sounded.

'What do you want? We're closing.'

'Can't you serve any more customers?'

'Nah. Too late. Go away.'

'But we're very hungry.'

I almost grinned. Yes, we were *very* hungry.

'Beat it!' Danny was in no mood for hospitality.

'Can't we get anything?'

Danny was silent for a moment. He was evidently debating the point. Then he called to someone inside the stand.

'Marie! Couple customers outside. Think we can fix 'em up in a hurry?'

'Oh, I guess so.' The girl's voice was soft, complaisant. Would she be soft and complaisant, too?

'Open up. You guys mind eating outside?'

'Not at all.'

'Open the door, Marie.'

Marie's high heels clattered across the wooden floor. She opened the screen door, blinked out into the darkness.

My companion stepped inside the doorway. Abruptly, he pushed the girl forward.

'Now!' he rasped.

I lunged at her in darkness. I didn't remember his instructions about smiling at her, or placing my hands beneath her ears. All I knew was that her throat was white, and smooth, except where a tiny vein throbbed in her neck.

I wanted to touch her neck there with my fingers – with my mouth – with my teeth.

So I dragged her into the darkness, and my hands were over her mouth, and I could hear her heels scraping through the gravel as I pulled her along. From inside the shack I heard a single long moan, and then nothing.

Nothing … except the rushing white blur of her neck, as my face swooped towards the throbbing vein …

IV

It was cold in the cellar – cold, and dark. I stirred uneasily on my couch and my eyes blinked open on blackness. I strained to see, raising myself to a sitting position as the chill slowly faded from my bones.

I felt sluggish, heavy with reptilian contentment. I yawned, trying to grasp a thread of memory from the red haze cloaking my thoughts.

Where was I? How had I come here? What had I been doing?

I yawned. One hand went to my mouth. My lips were caked with a dry, flaking substance.

I felt it – and then remembrance flooded me.

Last night, at the drive-in, I had feasted. And then –

'No!' I gasped.

'You have slept? Good.'

My host stood before me. I arose hastily and confronted him. 'Tell me it isn't true,' I pleaded. 'Tell me I was dreaming.'

'You were,' he answered. 'When I came out of the shack you lay under the trees, unconscious. I carried you home before dawn and placed you here to rest. You have been dreaming from sunrise to sunset, Graham Keene.'

'But last night – ?'

'Was real.'

'You mean I took that girl and – ?'

'Exactly.' He nodded. 'But come, we must go upstairs and talk. There are certain questions I must ask.'

We climbed the stairs slowly and emerged on ground level. Now I could observe my surroundings with a more objective eye. This house was large, and old. Although completely furnished, it looked somehow untenanted. It was as though nobody had lived here for a long time.

Then I remembered who my host was, and what he was. I smiled grimly. It was true. Nobody was *living* in this house now.

Dust lay thickly everywhere, and the spiders had spun patterns of decay in the corners. Shades were drawn against the darkness, but still it crept in through the cracked walls. For darkness and decay belonged here.

We entered the study where I had awakened last night, and as I was seated, my guardian cocked his head towards me in an attitude of inquiry.

'Let us speak frankly,' he began. 'I want you to answer an important question.'

'Yes?'

'What did you do with her?'

'Her?'

'That girl – last night. What did you do with her body?'

I put my hands to my temples. 'It was all a blur. I can't seem to remember.'

His head darted towards me, eyes blazing. 'I'll tell you what you did with her,' he rasped. 'You threw her body down the well. I saw it floating there.'

'Yes,' I groaned. 'I remember now.'

'You fool – why did you do that?'

'I wanted to hide it … I thought they'd never know – '

'You *thought!*' Scorn weighted his voice. 'You didn't think for an instant. Don't you see, now she will never rise?'

'Rise?'

'Yes, as you rose. Rise to become one of us.'

'But I don't understand.'

'That is painfully evident.' He paced the floor, then wheeled towards me.

'I see that I shall have to explain certain things to you. Perhaps you are not to blame, because you don't realize the situation. Come with me.'

He beckoned. I followed. We walked down the hall, entered a large, shelf-lined room. It was obviously a library. He lit a lamp, halted.

'Take a look around,' he invited. 'See what you make of it, my friend.'

I scanned the titles on the shelves – titles stamped in gold on thick, handsome bindings; titles worn to illegibility on ancient, raddled leather. The latest in scientific and medical treatises stood on these shelves, flanked by age-encrusted incunabula.

Modern volumes dealt with psychopathology. The ancient lore was frankly concerned with black magic.

'Here is the collection,' he whispered. 'Here is gathered together all that is known, all that has ever been written about – us.'

'A library on vampirism?'

'Yes. It took me decades to assemble it – completely.'

'But why?'

'Because knowledge is power. And it is power I seek.'

Suddenly a resurgent sanity impelled me. I shook off the nightmare enveloping me and sought an objective viewpoint. A question crept into my mind, and I did no try to hold it back.

'Just who are you, anyway?' I demanded. 'What is your name?'

My host smiled.

'I have no name,' he answered.

'No name?'

'Unfortunate, is it not? When I was buried, there were no loving friends, apparently, to erect a tombstone. And when I arose from the grave, I had no mentor to guide me back to a memory of the past. Those were barbaric times in the East Prussia of 1777.'

'You died in 1777?' I muttered.

'To the best of my knowledge,' he retorted, bowing slightly in mock deprecation. 'And so it is that my real name is unknown. Apparently I perished far from my native heath, for diligent research on my part has failed to uncover my paternity, or any contemporaries who recognized me at the time of my – er – resurrection.

'And so it is that I have no name; or rather, I have many pseudonyms. During the past sixteen decades I have travelled far, and have been all things to all men. I shall not endeavour to recite my history.

'It is enough to say that slowly, gradually, I have grown wise in the ways of the world. And I have evolved a plan. To this end I have amassed wealth, and brought together a library as a basis for my operations.

'Those operations I propose will interest you. And they will explain my anger when I think of you throwing the girl's body into the well.'

He sat down. I followed suit. I felt anticipation crawling along my spine. He was about to reveal something – something I wanted to hear, yet dreaded. The revelation came, slyly, slowly.

'Have you ever wondered,' he began, 'why there are not more vampires in the world?'

'What do you mean?'

'Consider. It is said, and it is true, that every victim of a vampire becomes a vampire in turn. The new vampire finds other victims. Isn't it reasonable to suppose, therefore, that in a short time – through sheer mathematical progression – the virus of vampirism would run epidemic throughout the world? In other words, have you ever wondered why the world is not filled with vampires by this time?'

'Well, yes – I never thought of it that way. What is the reason?' I asked

He glared and raised a white finger. It stabbed forward at my chest – a rapier of accusation.

'Because of fools like you. Fools who cast their victims into wells; fools whose victims are buried in sealed coffins, who hide the bodies or dismember them so no one would suspect their work.

'As a result, few new recruits join the ranks. And the old ones – myself included – are constantly subject to the ravages of the centuries. We eventually disintegrate, you know. To my knowledge, there are only a few hundred vampires today. And yet, if new victims all were given the opportunity to rise – we would have a vampire army within a year. Within three years there would be millions of vampires! Within ten years we could rule earth!

'Can't you see that? If there was no cremation, no careless disposal of bodies, no bungling, we could end our hunted existence as creatures of the night – brothers of the bat! No longer would we be a legendary, cowering minority, living each a law unto himself!

'All that is needed is a plan. And I – I have evolved that plan!'

His voice rose. So did the hairs upon my neck. I was

beginning to comprehend, now –

'Suppose we started with the humble instruments of destiny,' he suggested. 'Those forlorn, unnoticed, ignorant little old men – night watchmen of graveyards and cemeteries.'

A smile creased his corpse-like countenance. 'Suppose we eliminated them? Took over their jobs? Put vampires in their places – men who would go to the fresh graves and dig up the bodies of each victim they had bitten while those bodies were still warm and pulsing and undecayed?

'We could save the lives of most of the recruits we make. Reasonable, is it not?'

To me it was madness, but I nodded.

'Suppose that we made victims of those attendants? Then carried them off, nursed them back to reanimation, and allowed them to resume their posts as our allies? They work only at night – no one would know.

'Just a little suggestion, but so obvious! And it would mean so much!'

His smile broadened.

'All that it takes is organization on our part. I know many of my brethren. It is my desire soon to call them together and present this plan. Never before have we worked cooperatively, but when I show them the possibilities, they cannot fail to respond.

'Can you imagine it? An earth which we could control and terrorize – a world in which human beings become our property, our cattle?

'It is so simple, really. Sweep aside your foolish concepts of *Dracula* and the other superstitious confectionery that masquerades in the public mind as an authentic picture. I admit that we are – unearthly. But there is no reason for us to be stupid, impractical figures of fantasy. There is more for us than crawling around in black cloaks and recoiling at the sight of crucifixes!

'After all, we are a life-form, a race of our own. Biology has not yet recognized us, but we exist. Our morphology and metabolism has not been evacuated or charted; our actions and reactions never studied. But we exist. And we are superior to ordinary mortals. Let us assert this superiority! Plain human cunning, coupled with our super-normal powers, can create for us a mastery over all living things. For we are greater than Life – we are Life-in-Death!'

I half-rose. He waved me back, breathlessly.

'Suppose we band together and make plans? Suppose we go about, first of all, selecting our victims on the basis of value to our ranks? Instead of regarding them as sources of easy nourishment, let's think in terms of an army seeking recruits. Let us select keen brains, youthfully strong bodies. Let us prey upon the best earth has to offer. Then we shall wax strong and no man shall stay our hand – or teeth!'

He crouched like a black spider, spinning his web of words to enmesh my sanity. His eyes glittered. It was absurd somehow to see this creature of superstitious terror calmly creating a super-dictatorship of the dead.

And yet, I was one of them. It was real. The nameless one would do it, too.

'Have you ever stopped to wonder why I tell you this? Have you ever stopped to wonder why you are my confidant in this venture?' he purred.

I shook my head.

'It is because you are young. I am old. For years I have laboured only to this end. Now that my plans are perfected, I need assistance. Youth, a modern viewpoint. I know of you, Graham Keene. I watched you before ... you became one of us. You were selected for this purpose.'

'Selected?' Suddenly it hit home. I fought down a stranglehold gasp as I asked the question. 'Then you know who – did this to me? *You know who bit me?*'

Rotting fangs gaped in a smile. He nodded slowly.

'Of course,' he whispered. 'Why – *I* did!'

V

He was probably prepared for anything except the calmness with which I accepted this revelation.

Certainly he was pleased. And the rest of that night, and all the next night, were spent in going over the plans, in detail. I learned that he had not yet communicated with – others – in regard to his ideas.

A meeting would be arranged soon. Then we would begin the campaign. As he said, the times were ripe. War, a world in unrest – we would be able to move unchallenged and find unusual opportunities.

I agreed. I was even able to add certain suggestions as to detail. He was pleased with my cooperation.

Then, on the third night, came hunger.

He offered to serve as my guide, but I brushed him aside.

'Let me try my own wings,' I smiled. 'After all, I must learn sooner or later. This time I will see to it that the body remains intact. Then I shall discover the place of the burial and we can perform an experiment. I will select a likely recruit, we shall go forth to open the grave, and thus will we test our plan in miniature.'

He fairly beamed at that. And I went forth that night, alone.

I returned only as dawn welled out of the eastern sky – returned to slumber through the day.

That night we spoke, and I confided my success to his eager ears.

'Sidney J. Garrat is the name,' I said. 'A college professor, about 45. I found him wandering along a path near the campus. The trees form a dark, deserted avenue. He offered no resistance. I left him there. I don't think they'll bother with an autopsy – for the marks on his throat are invisible and he is known to have a weak heart.

'He lived alone without relatives. He had no money. That means a wooden coffin and quick burial at Everest tomorrow. Tomorrow night we can go there.'

My companion nodded.

'You have done well,' he said.

We spent the remainder of the night in perfecting our plans. We would go to Everest, locate the night watchman and put him out of the way, then seek the new grave of Professor Garrat.

And so it was that we re-entered the cemetery on the following evening.

Once again a midnight moon glared from the Cyclopean socket of the sky. Once more the wind whispered to us on our way, and the trees bowed in black obeisance along the path.

We crept to the shanty of the graveyard watchman and

peered through the window at his stooping figure.

'I'll knock,' I suggested. 'Then when he comes to the door – '

My companion shook his grey head. 'No teeth,' he whispered. 'The man is old, useless to us. I shall resort to more mundane weapons.'

I shrugged. Then I knocked. The old man opened the door, blinked out at me with rheumy eyes.

'What is it?' he wheezed, querulously. 'Ain't nobuddy suppose' tuh be in uh cemetery this time uh night – '

Lean fingers closed around his windpipe. My companion dragged him forth towards nearby shrubbery. His free arm rose and fell, and a silver arc stabbed down. He had used a knife.

Then we made haste along the path, before the scent of blood could divert us from our mission – and far head, on the hillside dedicated to the last slumbers of Poverty, I saw the raw, gaping edges of a new-made grave.

He ran back to the hut, then, and procured the spades we had neglected in our haste. The moon was our lantern and the grisly work began amidst a whistling wind.

No one saw us, no one heard us, for only empty eyes and shattered ears lay far beneath the earth.

We toiled, and then we stooped and tugged. The grave was deep, very deep. At the bottom the coffin lay, and we dragged forth the pine box.

'Terrible job,' confided my companion. 'Not a professionally dug grave at all, in my opinion. Wasn't filled in right. And this coffin is pine, but very thick. He'd never claw his way out. Couldn't break through the boards. And the earth was packed too tightly. Why would they waste so much time on a pauper's grave?'

'Doesn't matter,' I whispered. 'Let's open it up. If he's revived, we must hurry.'

We'd brought a hammer from the caretaker's shanty, too, and he went down into the pit itself to pry the nails free. I heard the board covering move, and peered down over the edge of the grave.

He bent forward, stooping to peer into the coffin, his face a mask of livid death in the moonlight. I heard him hiss.

'Why – the coffin is empty!' he gasped.

'Not for long!'

I drew the wrench from my pocket, raised it, brought it down with every ounce of strength I possessed until it shattered through his skull.

And then I leaped down into the pit and pressed the writhing, mewing shape down into the coffin, slammed the lid on, and drove the heavy nails into place. I could hear his whimperings rise to muffled screams, but the screams grew faint as I began to heap the clods of earth upon the coffin-lid.

I worked and panted there until no sound came from the coffin below. I packed the earth down hard – harder than I had last night when I dug the grave in the first place.

And then, at last, the task was over.

He lay there, the nameless one, the deathless one; lay six feet underground in a stout wooden coffin.

He could not claw his way free, I knew. And even if he did, I'd pressed him into his wooden prison face down. He'd claw his way to hell, not to earth.

But he was past escape. Let him lie there, as he had described it to me – not dead, not alive. Let him be conscious as he decayed, and as the wood decayed and the worms crawled in to feast. Let him suffer until the maggots at last reached his corrupt brain and ate away his evil consciousness.

I could have driven a stake through his heart. But his ghastly desire deserved defeat in this harsher fate.

Thus it was ended, and I could return now before discovery and the coming of dawn – return to his great house which was the only home I knew on the face of the earth.

Return I did, and for the past hours I have been writing this that all might know the truth.

I am not skilled with words, and what I read here smacks of mawkish melodrama. For the world is superstitious and yet cynical – and this account will be deemed the ravings of a fool or a madman; worse still, as a practical joke.

So I must implore you; if you seek to test the truth of what I've set down, go to Everest tomorrow and search out the newly-dug grave on the hillside. Talk to the police when they find the dead watchman, make them go to the well near

Danny's roadside stand.

Then, if you must, dig up the grave and find that which must still writhe and crawl within. When you see it, you'll believe – and in justice, you will not relieve the torment of that monstrous being by driving a stake through his heart.

For that stake represents release and peace.

I wish you'd come here, after that – and bring a stake for me ...

IX

The Screaming Woman

Ray Bradbury

Like Robert Bloch, fellow Californian Ray Bradbury (1920-) served his literary apprenticeship in the pages of Weird Tales *and over the years a number of his best stories have made excellent material for radio adaptations. Ray retains fond memories of the 'Golden Age' of broadcasting and indeed during the early 1940's wrote a number of radio scripts for Los Angeles stations – one memorable series appealing for blood donations for the Red Cross! Most appropriate, surely, for the man who created one of the most unusual families of vampires to be found anywhere in literature! When CBS launched their* Suspense *series in 1947, Ray was one of a number of writers approached to contribute, and he sold them several original stories which were aired during the next couple of years. They proved to be highlights of the programme because of their unusual themes among the many other much more traditional tales of mystery and crime. The best of them may well have been 'The Screaming Woman' which was broadcast in November 1948 and later turned by Ray into a fine short story which appears hereunder. Aside from several other contributions to* Suspense, *Ray's work has also been featured in the wholly Science Fiction series* Dimension X *(later retitled* X Minus 1*) which was launched in 1949 as the appeal of radio was beginning to decline under the onslaught of television, and in* Escape *(1950-3) and* Radio Workshop *(1953-6).*

My name is Margaret Leary and I'm ten years old and in the fifth grade at Central School. I haven't any brothers or sisters, but I've got a nice father and mother except they don't pay much attention to me. And anyway, we never thought we'd have anything to do with a murdered woman. Or almost, anyway.

When you're just living on a street like we live on, you don't think awful things are going to happen, like shooting or stabbing or burying people under the ground, practically in your back yard. And when it does happen you don't believe it. You just go on buttering your toast or baking a cake.

I got to tell you how it happened. It was a noon in the middle of July. It was hot and Mama said to me, 'Margaret, you go to the store and buy some ice cream. It's Saturday. Dad's home for lunch, so we'll have a treat.'

I ran out across the empty lot behind our house. It was a big lot, where kids had played baseball, and broken glass and stuff. And on my way back from the store with the ice cream I was just walking along, minding my own business, when all of a sudden it happened.

I heard the Screaming Woman.

I stopped and listened.

It was coming up out of the ground.

A woman was buried under the rocks and dirt and glass, and she was screaming, all wild and horrible, for someone to dig her out.

I just stood there, afraid. She kept screaming, muffled.

Then I started to run. I fell down, got up, and ran some more. I got in the screen door of my house and there was Mama, calm as you please, not knowing what I knew, that there was a real live woman buried out in the back of our house, just a hundred yards away, screaming bloody murder.

'Mama,' I said.

'Don't stand there with the ice cream,' said Mama.

'But, Mama,' I said.

'Put it in the icebox,' she said.

'Listen, Mama, there's a Screaming Woman in the empty lot.'

'And wash your hands,' said Mama.

'She was screaming and screaming … '

'Let's see, now, salt and pepper,' said Mama, far away.

'Listen to me,' I said loud. 'We got to dig her out. She's buried under tons and tons of dirt and if we don't dig her out, she'll choke up and die.'

'I'm certain she can wait until after lunch,' said Mama.

'Mama, don't you believe me?'

'Of course, dear. Now wash your hands and take this plate of meat in to your father.'

'I don't even know who she is or how she got there,' I said. 'But we got to help her before it's too late.'

'Good gosh,' said Mama. 'Look at this ice-cream. What did you do, just stand in the sun and let it melt?'

'Well, the empty lot … '

'Go on, now, scoot.'

I went into the dining room.

'Hi, Dad, there's a Screaming Woman in the empty lot.'

'I never knew a woman who didn't,' said Dad.

'I'm serious,' I said.

'You look very grave,' said Father.

'We've got to get picks and shovels and excavate, like for an Egyptian mummy,' I said.

'I don't feel like an archaeologist, Margaret,' said Father. 'Now, some nice cool October day, I'll take you up on that.'

'But we can't wait that long,' I almost screamed. My heart was bursting in me. I was excited and scared and afraid and here was Dad, putting meat on his plate, cutting and chewing and paying no attention.

'Dad?' I said.

'Mmmmm?' he said, chewing.

'Dad, you just gotta come out after lunch and help me,' I said. 'Dad, Dad, I'll give you all the money in my piggy bank!'

'Well,' said Dad. 'So it's a business proposition, is it? It must be important for you to offer your perfectly good money. How much money will you pay, by the hour?'

'I got five whole dollars it took me a year to save, and it's all yours.'

Dad touched my arm. 'I'm touched, I'm really touched. You want me to play with you and you're willing to pay for my time. Honest, Margaret, you make your old Dad feel like a piker. I don't give you enough time. Tell you what, after lunch, I'll come out and listen to your Screaming Woman, free of charge.'

'Will you, oh, will you, really?'

'Yes, ma'am, that's what I'll do,' said Dad. 'But you must promise me one thing?'

'What?'

'If I come out, you must eat all of your lunch first.'

'I promise,' I said.

'Okay.'

Mother came in and sat down and we started to eat.

'Not so fast,' said Mama.

I slowed down. Then I started eating fast again.

'You heard your mother,' said Dad.

'The Screaming Woman,' I said. 'We got to hurry.'

'I,' said Father, 'intend sitting here quietly and judiciously giving my attention first to my steak, then to my potatoes, and my salad, of course, and then to my ice cream, and after that to a long drink of iced coffee, if you don't mind. I may be a good hour at it. And another thing, young lady, if you mention her name, this Screaming Whatsis, once more at this table during lunch, I won't go out with you to hear her recital.'

'Yes, sir.'

'Is that understood?'

'Yes, sir,' I said.

Lunch was a million years long. Everybody moved in slow motion, like those films you see at the movies. Mama got up slow and down slow and forks and knives and spoons moved slow. Even the flies in the room were slow, And Dad's cheek muscles moved slow. It was so slow. I wanted to scream, 'Hurry! Oh, please, rush, get up, run around, come on out, run!'

But no, I had to sit, and all the while we sat there slowly, slowly eating our lunch, out there in the empty lot (I could hear her screaming in my mind. *Scream!*) was the Screaming Woman, all alone, while the world ate its lunch and the sun was hot and the lot was empty as the sky.

'There we are,' said Dad, finished at last.

'Now will you come out to see the Screaming Woman?' I said.

'First a little more iced coffee,' said Dad.

'Speaking of Screaming Women,' said Mother, 'Charlie Nesbitt and his wife Helen had another fight last night.'

'That's nothing new,' said Father. 'They're always fighting.'

'If you ask me, Charlie's no good,' said Mother. 'Or her either.'

'Oh, I don't know,' said Dad. 'I think she's pretty nice.'

'You're prejudiced. After all, you almost married her.'

'You going to bring that up again?' he said. 'After all, I was only engaged to her six weeks.'

'You showed some sense when you broke it off.'

'Oh, you know Helen. Always stagestruck. Wanted to travel in a trunk. I just couldn't see it. That broke it up. She was sweet, though. Sweet and kind.'

'What did it get her? A terrible brute of a husband like Charlie.'

'Dad,' I said.

'I'll give you that, Charlie has got a terrible temper,' said Dad. 'Remember when Helen had the lead in our high school graduation play? Pretty as a picture. She wrote some songs for it herself. That was the summer she wrote that song for me.'

'Ha,' said Mother.

'Don't laugh. It was a good song.'

'You never told me about that song.'

'It was between Helen and me. Let's see, how *did* it go?'

'Dad,' I said.

'You'd better take your daughter out in the back lot,' said Mother, 'before she collapses. You can sing me that wonderful song later.'

'Okay, come on, you,' said Dad, and I ran him out of the house.

The empty lot was still empty and hot and the glass sparkled green and white and brown all around where the bottles lay.

'Now, where's this Screaming Woman?' laughed Dad.

'We forgot the shovels,' I cried.

'We'll get them later, after we hear the soloist,' said Dad.

We listened.

'I don't hear anything,' said Dad, at last.

'Shh,' I said. 'Wait.'

We listened some more. 'Hey, there, Screaming Woman!' I cried.

We heard the sun in the sky. We heard the wind in the trees, real quiet. We heard a bus, far away, running along. We heard a car pass.

That was all.

'Margaret,' said Father. 'I suggest you go lie down and put a damp cloth on your forehead.'

'But she was here,' I shouted. 'I heard her, screaming, and screaming and screaming. See, here's where the ground's been dug up.' I called frantically at the earth. 'Hey, there, you down there!'

'Margaret,' said Father. 'This is the place where Mr Kelly dug yesterday, a big hole, to bury his trash and garbage in.'

'But during the night,' I said, 'someone else used Mr Kelly's burying place to bury a woman. And covered it all over again.'

'Well, I'm going back in and take a cool shower,' said Dad.

'You won't help me dig?'

'Better not stay out here too long,' said Dad. 'It's hot.'

Dad walked off. I heard the back door slam.

I stamped on the ground. 'Darn,' I said.

The screaming started again.

She screamed and screamed. Maybe she had been tired and was resting and now she began it all over, just for me.

I stood in the empty lot in the hot sun and I felt like crying. I ran back to the house and banged the door.

'Dad, she's screaming again!'

'Sure, sure,' said Dad. 'Come on.' And he led me to my upstairs bedroom. 'Here,' he said. He made me lie down and put a cold rag on my head. 'Just take it easy.'

I began to cry. 'Oh, Dad, we can't let her die. She's all buried, like that person in that story by Edgar Allan Poe, and think how awful it is to be screaming and no one paying any attention.'

'I forbid you to leave the house,' said Dad, worried. 'You just lie there the rest of the afternoon.' He went out and locked the door. I heard him and Mother talking in the front room. After a while I stopped crying. I got up and tiptoed to the window. My room was upstairs. It seemed high.

I took a sheet off the bed and tied it to the bedpost and let it out the window. Then I climbed out the window and shinnied down until I touched the ground. Then I ran to the garage, quiet, and I got a couple of shovels and I ran to the empty lot. It was hotter than ever. And I started to dig, and all the while I dug, the Screaming Woman screamed ...

It was hard work. Shoving in the shovel and lifting the rocks and glass. And I knew I'd be doing it all afternoon and maybe I wouldn't finish in time. What could I do? Run tell other people? But they'd be like Mom and Dad, pay no attention. I just kept digging, all by myself.

About ten minutes later, Dippy Smith came along the path through the empty lot. He's my age and goes to my school.

'Hi. Margaret,' he said.

'Hi, Dippy,' I gasped.

'What you doing?' he asked.

'Digging.'

'For what?'

'I got a Screaming Lady in the ground and I'm digging for her,' I said.

'I don't hear no screaming,' said Dippy.

'You sit down and wait awhile and you'll hear her scream yet. Or better still, help me dig.'

'I don't dig unless I hear a scream,' he said.

We waited.

'Listen!' I cried. 'Did you *hear* it?'

'Hey,' said Dippy, with slow appreciation, his eyes gleaming. 'That's okay. Do it again.'

'Do what again?'

'The scream.'

'We got to wait,' I said, puzzled.

'Do it again,' he insisted, shaking my arm. 'Go on.' He dug in his pocket for a brown aggie. 'Here.' He shoved it at me. 'I'll give you this marble if you do it again.'

A scream came out of the ground.

'Hot dog!' said Dippy. 'Teach *me* to do it!' He danced around as if I was a miracle.

'I don't … ' I started to say.

'Did you get the *Throw-Your-Voice* book for a dime from the Magic Company in Dallas, Texas?' cried Dippy. 'You got one of those tin ventriloquist contraptions in your mouth?'

'Y-yes,' I lied, for I wanted him to help. 'If you'll help me dig, I'll tell you about it later.'

'Swell,' he said. 'Give me a shovel.'

We both dug together, and from time to time the woman screamed.

'Boy,' said Dippy. 'You'd think she was right under foot. You're wonderful, Maggie.' Then he said, 'What's her name?'

'Who?'

'The Screaming Woman. You must have a name for her.'

'Oh, sure.' I thought a moment. 'Her name's Wilma Schweiger and she's a rich old woman, ninety-six years old, and she was buried by a man named Spike, who counterfeited ten-dollar bills.'

'Yes, *sir*,' said Dippy.

'And there's hidden treasure buried with her, and I, I'm a grave robber come to dig her out and get it,' I gasped, digging excitedly.

Dippy made his eyes Oriental and mysterious. 'Can I be a grave robber, too?' He had a better idea. 'Let's pretend it's the Princess Ommanatra, an Egyptian queen, covered with diamonds!'

We kept digging and I thought, Oh, we will rescue her, we *will*. If only we keep on!

'Hey, I just got an idea,' said Dippy. And he ran off and got a piece of cardboard. He scribbled on it with crayon.

'Keep digging!' I said. 'We can't stop!'

'I'm making a sign. See? SLUMBERLAND CEMETERY! We can bury some birds and beetles here, in matchboxes and stuff. I'll go find some butterflies.'

'No, Dippy!'

'It's more fun that way. I'll get me a dead cat, too, maybe … '

'Dippy, use your shovel! Please!'

'Aw,' said Dippy. 'I'm tired. I think I'll go home and take a nap.'

'You can't do that.'

'Who says so?'

'Dippy, there's something I want to tell you.'

'What?'

He gave the shovel a kick.

I whispered in his ear. 'There's really a woman buried here.'

'Why sure there is,' he said. 'You said it, Maggie.'

'You don't believe me, either.'

'Tell me how you throw your voice and I'll keep on digging.'

'But I can't tell you, because I'm not doing it,' I said. 'Look, Dippy, I'll stand way over here and you listen there.'

The Screaming Woman screamed again.

'Hey!' said Dippy. 'There really *is* a woman here!'

'That's what I tried to say.'

'Let's dig!' said Dippy.

We dug for twenty minutes.

'I wonder who she is?'

'I don't know.'

'I wonder if it's Mrs Nelson or Mrs Turner or Mrs Bradley. I wonder if she's pretty. Wonder what colour her hair is? Wonder if she's thirty or ninety or sixty?'

'Dig!' I said.

The mound grew high.

'Wonder if she'll reward us for digging her up.'

'Sure.'

'A quarter, do you think?'

'More than that. I bet it's a dollar.'

Dippy remembered as he dug, 'I read a book once of magic. There was a Hindu with no clothes on who crept down in a grave and slept there sixty days, not eating anything, no malts, no chewing gum or candy, no air, for sixty days.' His face fell. 'Say, wouldn't it be awful if it was only a radio buried here and us working so hard?'

'A radio's nice, it'd be all ours.'

Just then a shadow fell across us.

'Hey, you kids, what you think you're doing?'

We turned. It was Mr Kelly, the man who owned the empty lot. 'Oh, hello, Mr Kelly,' we said.

'Tell you what I want you to do,' said Mr Kelly. 'I want you to take those shovels and take that soil and shovel it right back in that hole you been digging. That's what I want you to do.'

My heart started beating fast again. I wanted to scream myself.

'But Mr Kelly, there's a Screaming Woman and ... '

'I'm not interested. I don't hear a thing.'

'Listen!' I cried.

The scream.

Mr Kelly listened and shook his head. 'Don't hear nothing. Go on now, fill it up and get home with you before I give you my foot!'

We filled the hole all back in again. And all the while we filled it, Mr Kelly stood there, arms folded, and the woman screamed, but Mr Kelly pretended not to hear it.

When we were finished, Mr Kelly stomped off, saying, 'Go on home now. And if I catch you here again … '

I turned to Dippy. 'He's the one,' I whispered.

'Huh?' said Dippy.

'He *murdered* Mrs Kelly. He buried her here, after he strangled her, in a box, but she came to. Why, he stood right here and she screamed and he wouldn't pay any attention.'

'Hey,' said Dippy. 'That's right. He stood right here and lied to us.'

'There's only one thing to do,' I said. 'Call the police and have them arrest Mr Kelly.'

We ran for the corner store telephone.

The police knocked on Mr Kelly's door five minutes later. Dippy and I were hiding in the bushes, listening.

'Mr Kelly?' said the police officer.

'Yes, sir, what can I do for you?'

'Is Mrs Kelly at home?'

'Yes, sir.'

'May we see her, sir?'

'Of course. Hey, Anna!'

Mrs Kelly came to the door and looked out. 'Yes, sir?'

'I beg your pardon,' apologized the officer. 'We had a report that you were buried out in an empty lot, Mrs Kelly. It sounded like a child made the call, but we had to be certain. Sorry to have troubled you.'

'It's those blasted kids,' cried Mr Kelly, angrily. 'If I ever catch them, I'll rip them limb from limb!'

'Cheezit!' said Dippy, and we both ran.

'What'll we do now?' I said.

'I got to go home,' said Dippy. 'Boy, we're really in trouble. We'll get a licking for this.'

'But what about the Screaming Woman?'

'To heck with her,' said Dippy. 'We don't dare go near that empty lot again. Old man Kelly'll be waiting around with his razor strap and lambast heck out'n us. And I just happened to remember, Maggie. Ain't old man Kelly sort of deaf, hard-of-hearing?'

'Oh, my gosh,' I said. 'No *wonder* he didn't hear the screams.'

'So long,' said Dippy. 'We sure got in trouble over your darn old ventriloquist voice. I'll be seeing you.'

I was left all alone in the world, no one to help me, no one to believe me at all. I just wanted to crawl down in that box with the Screaming Woman and die. The police were after me now, for lying to them, only I didn't know it was a lie, and my father was probably looking for me, too, or would be once he found my bed empty. There was only one last thing to do, and I did it.

I went from house to house, all down the street, near the empty lot. And I rang every bell and when the door opened I said: 'I beg your pardon, Mrs Griswold, but is anyone missing from your house?' or 'Hello, Mrs Pikes, you're looking fine today. Glad to see you *home*.' And once I saw that the lady of the house was home I just chatted awhile to be polite, and went on down the street.

The hours were rolling along. It was getting late. I kept thinking, oh, there's only so much air in that box with that woman under the earth, and if I don't hurry, she'll suffocate, and I got to rush! So I rang bells and knocked on doors, and it got later, and I was just about to give up and go home, when I knocked on the *last* door, which was the door of Mr Charlie Nesbitt, who lives next to us. I kept knocking and knocking.

Instead of Mrs Nesbitt, or Helen as my father calls her, coming to the door, why it was Mr Nesbitt, Charlie, *himself*.

'Oh,' he said. 'It's you, Margaret.'

'Yes,' I said. 'Good afternoon.'

'What can I do for you, kid?' he said.

'Well, I thought I'd like to see your wife, Mrs Nesbitt,' I said.

'Oh,' he said.

'May I?'

'Well, she's gone out to the store,' he said.

'I'll wait,' I said, and slipped in past him.

'Hey,' he said.

I sat down in a chair. 'My, it's a hot day,' I said, trying to be calm, thinking about the empty lot and air going out of the box, and the screams getting weaker and weaker.

'Say, listen, kid,' said Charlie, coming over to me, 'I don't think you better wait.'

'Oh, sure,' I said. 'Why not?'

'Well, my wife won't be back,' he said.

'Oh?'

'Not today, that is. She's gone to the store, like I said, but, but, she's going on from there to visit her mother. Yeah. She's going to visit her mother, in Schenectady. She'll be back, two or three days, maybe a week.'

'That's a shame,' I said.

'Why?'

'I wanted to tell her something.'

'What?'

'I just wanted to tell her there's a woman buried over in the empty lot, screaming under tons and tons of dirt.'

Mr Nesbitt dropped his cigarette.

'You dropped your cigarette, Mr Nesbitt,' I pointed out, with my shoe.

'Oh, did I? Sure, so I did,' he mumbled. 'Well, I'll tell Helen when she comes home, your story. She'll be glad to hear it.'

'Thanks. It's a real woman.'

'How do you know it is?'

'I heard her.'

'How, how you know it isn't, well, a *mandrake* root?'

'What's that?'

'You know. A mandrake. It's a kind of plant, kid. They scream. I know, I read it once. How you know it ain't a mandrake?'

'I never thought of that.'

'You better start thinking,' he said, lighting another cigarette. He tried to be casual. 'Say, kid, you, eh, you *say* anything about this to anyone?'

'Sure. I told lots of people.'

Mr Nesbitt burned his hand on his match.

'Anybody doing anything about it?' he asked.

'No,' I said. 'They won't believe me.'

He smiled. 'Of course. Naturally. You're nothing but a kid. Why should they listen to you?'

'I'm going back now and dig her out with a spade,' I said.

'Wait.'

'I got to go,' I said.

'Stick around,' he insisted.

'Thanks, but no,' I said, frantically.

He took my arm. 'Know how to play cards, kid? Black jack?'
'Yes, sir.'
He took out a deck of cards from a desk. 'We'll have a game.'
'I got to go dig.'
'Plenty of time for that,' he said, quiet. 'Anyway, maybe my wife'll be home. Sure. that's it. You wait for her. Wait awhile.'
'You think she will be?'
'Sure, kid. Say, about that voice; is it very strong?'
'It gets weaker all the time.'
Mr Nesbitt sighed and smiled. 'You and your kid games. Here now, let's play that game of black jack, it's more fun than Screaming Women.'
'I got to go. It's late.'
'Stick around, you got nothing to do.'
I knew what he was trying to do. He was trying to keep me in his house until the screaming died down and was gone. He was trying to keep me from helping her. 'My wife'll be home in ten minutes,' he said. 'Sure. Ten minutes. You wait. You sit right there.'
We played cards. The clock ticked. The sun went down the sky. It was getting late. The screaming got fainter and fainter in my mind. 'I got to go,' I said.
'Another game,' said Mr Nesbitt. 'Wait another hour, kid. My wife'll come yet. Wait.'
In another hour he looked at his watch. 'Well, kid, I guess you can go now.' And I knew what his plan was. He'd sneak down in the middle of the night and dig up his wife, still alive, and take her somewhere else and bury her, good. 'So long, kid. So long.' He let me go, because he thought that by now the air must all be gone from the box.
The door shut in my face.
I went back near the empty lot and hid in some bushes. What could I do? Tell my folks? But they hadn't believed me. Call the police on Mr Charlie Nesbitt? But he said his wife was away visiting. Nobody would believe me!
I watched Mr Kelly's house. He wasn't in sight. I ran over to the place where the screaming had been and just stood there.
The screaming had stopped. It was so quiet I thought I would never hear a scream again. It was all over. I was too late, I thought.

I bent down and put my ear to the ground.

And then I heard it, way down, way deep, and so faint I could hardly hear it.

The woman wasn't screaming any more. She was singing.

Something about, 'I loved you fair, I loved you well.'

It was sort of a sad song. Very faint. And sort of broken. All of those hours down under the ground in that box must have sort of made her crazy. All she needed was some air and food and she'd be all right. But she just kept singing, not wanting to scream any more, not caring, just singing.

I listened to the song.

And then I turned and walked straight across the lot and up the steps to my house and I opened the front door.

'Father,' I said.

'So there you are!' he cried.

'Father,' I said.

'You're going to get a licking,' he said.

'She's not screaming any more.'

'Don't talk about her!'

'She's singing now,' I cried.

'You're not telling the truth!'

'Dad,' I said. 'She's out there and she'll be dead soon if you don't listen to me. She's out there, singing, and this is what she's singing.' I hummed the tune. I sang a few of the words. 'I loved you fair, I loved you well ... '

Dad's face grew pale. He came and took my arm.

'What did you say?' he said.

I sang it again: 'I loved you fair, I loved you well.'

'Where did you *hear* that song?' he shouted.

'Out in the empty lot, just now.'

'But that's *Helen's* song, the one she wrote, years ago, for *me*!' cried Father. 'You *can't* know it. *Nobody* knew it, except Helen and me. I never sang it to anyone, not you or anyone.'

'Sure,' I said.

'Oh, my God!' cried Father, and ran out the door to get a shovel. The last I saw of him he was in the empty lot, digging, and lots of other people with him, digging.

I felt so happy I wanted to cry.

I dialled a number on the phone and when Dippy answered I said, 'Hi, Dippy. Everything's fine. Everything's worked out keen. The Screaming Woman isn't screaming any more.'

'Swell,' said Dippy.

'I'll meet you in the empty lot with a shovel in two minutes,' I said.

'Last one there's a monkey! So long!' cried Dippy.

'So long, Dippy!' I said, and ran.

X

The Other Hangman

John Dickson Carr

The bleak years of the early 1940's, when Britain was engulfed in the struggles of the Second World War, heralded the arrival on radio of one of the most successful and still best remembered series ever broadcast in the country – Appointment With Fear. Despite the grimness of everyday life, the stories which made up the series provided such outstanding 'escapist' listening that the show became a must for many thousands every week. An important feature of this success was the telling of the stories by the slightly sinister host known simply as 'The Man in Black'. The unmistakable voice of this man belonged to the actor Valentine Dyall, and such was its impact that the tones remain a vivid memory to a great many people even now. Dyall, for his part, is still busy as a character actor, primarily in television. Credit is also due in no small measure to the man who wrote the scripts, the American mystery story writer, John Dickson Carr (1906-1977) of whom J.B.Priestley declared, 'He possesses a sense of the macabre that lifts him high above the average run of writers.' Born the son of a United States Congressman, Carr had married an English girl and settled in England shortly before the outbreak of hostilities. He had grown up loving creepy stories – recalling being told them on the knees of his Uncle Joe Cannon when he was only eight years old – and his creation of Appointment With Fear for the BBC proved to be one of the great wartime broadcasting successes and it continued until 1953. It is also interesting to discover that when Carr, who had never renounced his citizenship, returned to America in 1942 in order to be called up for service in the Armed Forces, such was the popularity of Appointment With Fear that the BBC requested his return – and this was in fact duly granted by the American authorities! A considerable number of the tales that Carr wrote for 'The Man In Black' were based on his own short stories, and the example that follows, 'The Other Hangman', is, I think, among the most memorable. After all, what more terrible appointment could there be than with this man?

'Why do they electrocute 'em instead of hanging 'em in Pennsylvania? What' (said my old friend, Judge Murchison, dexterously hooking the spittoon closer with his foot) 'do they teach you youngsters in these new-fangled law schools, anyway? That, son, *was* a murder case. It turned the Supreme Court's whiskers grey to find a final ruling, and for thirty years it's been argued about by lawyers in the back room of every saloon from here to the Pacific coast. It happened right here in this county – when they hanged Fred Joliffe for the murder of Randall Fraser.

'It was in '92 or '93; anyway, it was the year they put the first telephone in the court-house, and you could talk as far as Pittsburg except when the wires blew down. Considering it was the county seat, we were mighty proud of our town (population 3,500). The hustlers were always bragging about how thriving and growing our town was, and we had just got to the point of enthusiasm where every ten years we were certain the census-taker must have forgotten half our population. Old Mark Sturgis, who owned the *Bugle Gazette* then, carried on something awful in an editorial when they printed in the almanac that we had a population of only 3,265. We were all pretty riled about it, naturally.

'We were proud of plenty of other things, too. We had good reason to brag about the McClellan House, which was the finest hotel in the county; and I mind when you could get a room and board, with apple pie for breakfast every morning, for two dollars a week. We were proud of our old county families, that came over the mountains when Braddock's army was scalped by the Indians in seventeen fifty-five, and settled down in log huts to dry their wounds. But most of all we were proud of our legal batteries.

'Son, it was a grand assembly! Mind, I won't say that all of 'em were long on knowledge of the Statute Books; but they knew their *Blackstone* and their *Greenleaf on Evidence*, and they were powerful speakers. *And* there were some – the top-notchers

– full of graces and book-knowledge and dignity, who were hell on the exact letter of the law. Scotch-Irish Presbyterians, all of us, who loved a good debate and a bottle o' whisky. There was Charley Connell, a Harvard graduate and the district attorney, who had fine white hands, and wore a fine high collar, and made such pathetic addresses to the jury that people flocked for miles around to hear him; though he generally lost his cases. There was Judge Hunt, who prided himself on his resemblance to Abe Lincoln, and in consequence always wore a frock coat and an elegant plug hat. Why, there was your own grandfather, who had over two hundred books in his library, and people used to go up nights to borrow volumes of the encyclopaedia.

'You know the big stone court-house at the top of the street, with the flowers round it, and the jail adjoining? People went there as they'd go to a picture-show nowadays; it was a lot better, too. Well, from there it was only two minutes' walk across the meadow to Jim Riley's saloon. All the cronies gathered there – in the back room of course, where Jim had an elegant brass spittoon and a picture of George Washington on the wall to make it dignified. You could see the footpath worn across the grass until they built over that meadow. Besides the usual crowd, there was Bob Moran, the sheriff, a fine, strapping big fellow, but very nervous about doing his duty strictly. And there was poor old Nabors, a big, quiet, reddish-eyed fellow, who'd been a doctor before he took to drink. He was always broke, and he had two daughters – one of 'em consumptive – and Jim Riley pitied him so much that he gave him all he wanted to drink for nothing. Those were fine, happy days, with a power of eloquence and theorizing and solving the problems of the nation in that back room, until our wives came to fetch us home.

'Then Randall Fraser was murdered, and there was hell to pay.

'Now if it had been anybody else but Fred Joliffe who killed him, naturally we wouldn't have convicted. You can't do it, son, not in a little community. It's all very well to talk about the power and grandeur of justice, and sounds fine in a speech. But here's somebody you've seen walking the streets about his business every day for years; and you know when his kids were born, and saw him crying when one of 'em died; and you remember how he loaned you ten dollars when you needed it ... Well, you can't take that person out in the cold light of day and string him up by the neck until he's dead. You'd always be seeing the look on his face afterwards. And you'd find excuses for him no matter what he did.

'But with Fred Joliffe it was different. Fred Joliffe was the worst and nastiest customer we ever had, with the possible exception of Randall Fraser himself. Ever seen a copperhead curled up on a flat stone? And a copperhead's worse than a rattlesnake – that won't strike unless you step on it, and gives warning before it does. Fred Joliffe had the same brownish colour and sliding movements. You always remembered his pale little eye and his nasty grin. When he drove his cart through town – he had some sort of rag-and-bone business, you understand – you'd see him sitting up there, a skinny little man in a brown coat, peeping round the side of his nose to find something for gossip. And grinning.

'It wasn't merely the things he said about people behind their backs. Or to their faces, for that matter, because he relied on the fact that he was too small to be thrashed. He was a slick customer. It was believed that he wrote those anonymous letters that caused ... but never mind that. Anyhow, I can tell you his little smirk *did* drive Will Farmer crazy one time, and Will *did* beat him within an inch of his life. Will's livery stable was burnt down one night about a month later, with eleven horses inside, but nothing could ever be proved. He was too smart for us.

'That brings me to Fred Joliffe's only companion – I don't mean friend. Randall Fraser had a harness-and-saddle store in Market Street, a dusty place with a big dummy horse in the window. I reckon the only thing in the world Randall liked was that dummy horse, which was a dappled mare with vicious-looking glass eyes. He used to keep its mane combed. Randall was a big man with a fine moustache, a horseshoe pin in his tie, and sporty checked clothes. He was buttery polite, and mean as sin. He thought a dirty trick or a swindle was the funniest joke he ever heard. But the women liked him – a lot of them, it's no use denying, sneaked in at the back door of that harness store. Randall itched to tell it at the barber shop, to

show what fools they were and how virile he was; but he had to
be careful. He and Fred Joliffe did a lot of drinking together.

'Then the news came. It was in October, I think, and I heard
it in the morning when I was putting on my hat to go down to
the office. Old Withers was the town constable then. He got up
early in the morning, although there was no need for it; and,
when he was going down Market Street in the mist about five
o'clock, he saw the gas still burning in the back room of
Randall's store. The front door was wide open. Withers went in
and found Randall lying on a pile of harness in his
shirt-sleeves, and his forehead and face bashed in with a
wedging-mallet. There wasn't much left of the face, but you
could recognize him by his moustache and his horseshoe pin.

'I was in my office when somebody yelled up from the street
that they had found Fred Joliffe drunk and asleep in the
flour-mill, with blood on his hands and an empty bottle of
Randall Fraser's whisky in his pocket. He was still in bad
shape, and wouldn't walk or understand what was going on,
when the sheriff – that was Bob Moran I told you about – came
to take him to the lock-up. Bob had to drive him in his own
rag-and-bone cart. I saw them drive up Market Street in the
rain, Fred lying in the back of the cart all white with flour, and
rolling and cursing. People were very quiet. They were pleased,
but they couldn't show it.

'That is, all except Will Farmer, who had owned the livery
stable that was burnt down.

' "Now they'll hang him," says Will. "*Now*, by God, they'll
hang him."

'It's a funny thing, son: I didn't realize the force of that until
I heard Judge Hunt pronounce sentence after the trial. They
appointed me to defend him, because I was a young man
without any particular practice, and somebody had to do it.
The evidence was all over town before I got a chance to speak
with Fred. You could see he was done for. A scissors-grinder
who lived across the street (I forget his name now) had seen
Fred go into Randall's place about eleven o'clock. An old
couple who lived up over the store had heard 'em drinking and
yelling downstairs; at near on midnight they'd heard a noise
like a fight and a fall; but they knew better than to interfere.
Finally, a couple of farmers driving home from town at

midnight had seen Fred stumble out of the front door, slapping his clothes and wiping his hands on his coat like a man with delirium tremens.

'I went to see Fred at the jail. He was sober, although he jerked a good deal. Those pale watery eyes of his were as poisonous as ever. I can still see him sitting on the bunk in his cell, sucking a brown paper cigarette, wriggling his neck, and jeering at me. He wouldn't tell me anything, because he said I would go and tell the judge if he did.

' "Hang *me?*" he says, and wrinkled his nose and jeered again. "Hang *me?* Don't you worry about that, mister. Them so-and-so's will never hang me. They're too much afraid of me, them so-and-so's are. Eh, mister?"

'And the fool couldn't get it through his head right up until the sentence. He strutted away in court; making smart remarks, and threatening to tell what he knew about people, and calling the judge by his first name. He wore a new dickey shirt-front he bought to look spruce in.

'I was surprised how quietly everybody took it. The people who came to the trial didn't whisper or shove; they just sat still as death and looked at him. All you could hear was a kind of breathing. It's funny about a court-room, son: it has its own particular smell, which won't bother you unless you get to thinking about what it means, but you notice worn places and cracks in the walls more than you would anywhere else. You would hear Charley Connell's voice for the prosecution, a little thin sound in a big room, and Charley's footsteps creaking. You would hear a cough in the audience, or a woman's dress rustle, or the gas-jets whistling. It was dark in the rainy season, so they lit the gas-jets by two o'clock in the afternoon.

'The only defence I could make was that Fred had been too drunk to be responsible, and remembered nothing of that night (which he admitted was true). But, in addition to being no defence in law, it was a terrible frost besides. My own voice sounded wrong. I remember that six of the jury had whiskers and six hadn't; and Judge Hunt, up on the bench with the flag draped on the wall behind his head, looked more like Abe Lincoln than ever. Even Fred Joliffe began to notice. He kept twitching round to look at the people, a little uneasy-like. Once he stuck out his neck at the jury and screeched: "*Say* something, cantcha? Do something, cantcha?"

'They did.

'When the foreman of the jury said, "Guilty of murder in the first degree," there was just a little noise from those people. Not a cheer, or anything like that. It hissed out all together, only once, like breath released, but it was terrible to hear. It didn't hit Fred until Judge Hunt was half way through pronouncing sentence. Fred stood looking round with a wild, half-witted expression until he heard Judge Hunt say, *"And may God have mercy on your soul."* Then he burst out, kind of pleading and kidding as though this was carrying the joke too far. He said, "Listen, now, you don't *mean* that, do you? You can't fool me. You're only Jerry Hunt; I know who you are. You can't do that to me." All of a sudden he began pounding the table and screaming: "You ain't really agoing to hang me, are you?"

'But we were.

'The date of execution was fixed for the twelfth of November. The order was all signed. " ... within the precincts of the said county jail, between the hours of eight and nine A.M., the said Frederick Joliffe shall be hanged by the neck until he is dead; an executioner to be commissioned by the sheriff for this purpose, and the sentence to be carried out in the presence of a qualified medical practitioner; the body to be interred ... " And the rest of it. Everybody was nervous. There hadn't been a hanging since any of that crowd had been in office, and nobody knew how to go about it exactly. Old Doc Macdonald, the coroner, was to be there; and of course they got hold of Reverend Phelps the preacher; and Bob Moran's wife was going to cook pancakes and sausage for the last breakfast. Maybe you think that's fool talk. But think for a minute of taking somebody you've known all your life, and binding his arms one cold morning, and walking him out in your own backyard to crack his neck on a rope – all religious and legal, with not a soul to interfere. Then you begin to get scared of the powers of life and death, and the thin partition between.

'Bob Moran was scared white for fear things wouldn't go off properly. He had appointed big, slow-moving, tipsy Ed Nabors as hangman. This was partly because Ed Nabors

needed the fifty dollars that was the fee, and partly because Bob
had a vague idea that an ex-medical man would be better able to
manage an execution. Ed had sworn to keep sober; Bob Moran
said he wouldn't get a dime unless he *was* sober; but you
couldn't always tell.

'Nabors seemed in earnest. He had studied up the matter of
scientific hanging in an old book he borrowed from your
grandfather, and he and the carpenter had knocked together a
big, shaky-looking contraption in the jail yard. It worked all
right in practice, with sacks of meal; the trap went down with a
boom that brought your heart up in your throat. But once they
allowed for too much spring in the rope, and it tore a sack apart.
Then old Doc Macdonald chipped in about that fellow John
Lee, in England – and it nearly finished Bob Moran.

'That was late on the night before the execution. We were
sitting round the lamp in Bob's office, trying to play stud poker.
There were tops and skipping-ropes, all kinds of toys, all over
that office. Bob let his kids play in there – which he shouldn't
have done, because the door out of it led to a corridor of cells
with Fred Joliffe in the last one. Of course the few other
prisoners, disorderlies and chicken-thieves and the like, had
been moved upstairs. Somebody had told Bob that the scent of
an execution affects 'em like a cage of wild animals. Whoever it
was, he was right. We could hear 'em shifting and stamping over
our heads, and one old nigger singing hymns all night long.

'Well, it was raining hard on the tin roof; maybe that was what
put Doc Macdonald in mind of it. Doc was a cynical old devil.
When he saw that Bob couldn't sit still, and would throw in his
hand without even looking at the buried card, Doc says:

' "Yes, I hope it'll go off all right. But you want to be careful
about that rain. Did you read about that fellow they tried to
hang in England? – and the rain had swelled the boards so's the
trap wouldn't fall? They stuck him on it three times, but still it
wouldn't work … "

'Ed Nabors slammed his hand down on the table. I reckon he
felt bad enough as it was, because one of his daughters had run
away and left him, and the other was dying of consumption. But
he was twitchy and reddish about the eyes; he hadn't had a drink
for two days, although there was a bottle on the table. He says:

' "You shut up or I'll kill you. Damn you, Macdonald," he

says, and grabs the edge of the table. "I tell you nothing *can* go wrong. I'll go out and test the thing again, if you'll let me put the rope round your neck."

'And Bob Moran says: "What do you want to talk like that for anyway, Doc? Ain't it bad enough as it is?" he says. "Now you've got me worrying about something else," he says. "I went down there a while ago to look at him, and he said the funniest thing I ever heard Fred Joliffe say. He's crazy. He giggled and said God wouldn't let them so-and-so's hang him. It was terrible, hearing Fred Joliffe talk like that. What time is it, somebody?"

'I was cold that night. I dozed off in a chair, hearing the rain, and that animal-cage snuffing upstairs. The nigger was singing that part of the hymn about while the nearer waters roll, while the tempest still is high.

'They woke me about half past eight to say that Judge Hunt and all the witnesses were out in the jail yard, and they were ready to start the march. Then I realized that they were really going to hang him after all. I had to join behind the procession as I was sworn, but I didn't see Fred Joliffe's face and I didn't want to see it. They had given him a good wash, and a clean flannel shirt that they tucked under at the neck. He stumbled coming out of the cell, and started to go in the wrong direction; but Bob Moran and the constable each had him by one arm. It was a cold, dark, windy morning. His hands were tied behind.

'The preacher was saying something I couldn't catch; everything went off smoothly enough until they got half-way across the jail yard. It's a pretty big yard. I didn't look at the contraption in the middle, but at the witnesses standing over against the wall with their hats off; and I smelled the clean air after the rain, and looked up at the mountains where the sky was getting pink. But Fred Joliffe did look at it, and went down flat on his knees. They hauled him up again. I heard them keep on walking, and go up the steps, which were creaky.

'I didn't look at the contraption until I heard a thumping sound, and we all knew something was wrong.

'Fred Joliffe was not standing on the trap, nor was the bag pulled over his head, although his legs were strapped. He stood with his eyes closed and his face towards the pink sky. Ed

Nabors was clinging with both hands to the rope, twirling round a little and stamping on the trap. It didn't budge. Just as I heard Ed crying something about the rain having swelled the boards, Judge Hunt ran past me to the foot of the contraption.

'Bob Moran started cursing pretty obscenely. "Put him on and try it, anyway," he says, and grabs Fred's arm. "Stick that bag over his head and give the thing a chance."

' "In His Name," says the preacher pretty steadily, "You'll not do it if I can help it."

"Bob ran over like a crazy man and jumped on the trap with both feet. It was stuck fast. Then Bob turned round and pulled an Ivor-Johnson .45 out of his hip-pocket. Judge Hunt got in front of Fred, whose lips were moving a little.

' "He'll have the law, and nothing but the law," says Judge Hunt. "Put that gun away, you lunatic, and take him back to the cell until you can make the thing work. Easy with him, now."

'To this day I don't think Fred Joliffe had realized what happened. I believe he only had his belief confirmed that they never meant to hang him after all. When he found himself going down the steps again, he opened his eyes. His face looked shrunken and dazed-like, but all of a sudden it came to him in a blaze.

' "I knew them so-and-so's would never hang me," says he. His throat was so dry he couldn't spit at Judge Hunt, as he tried to do; but he marched straight and giggling across the yard. "I knew them so-and-so's would never hang me," he says.

'We all had to sit down a minute, and we had to give Ed Nabors a drink. Bob made him hurry up, although we didn't say much, and he was leaving to fix the trap again when the court-house janitor came bustling into Bob's office.

' "Call," says he, "on the new machine over there. Telephone."

' "Lemme out of here!" yells Bob. "I can't listen to no telephone calls now. Come out and give us a hand."

' "But it's from Harrisburg," says the janitor. "It's from the Governor's office. You got to go."

' "Stay here, Bob," says Judge Hunt. He beckons to me. "Stay here, and I'll answer it," he says. We looked at each other in a queer way when we went across the Bridge of Sighs. The court-house clock was striking nine, and I could look down into the yard and see people hammering at the trap. After Judge Hunt had listened to that telephone call he had a hard time putting the receiver back on the hook.

' "I always believed in Providence, in a way," says he, "but I never thought it was so personal-like. Fred Joliffe is innocent. We're to call off this business,' says he, 'and wait for a messenger from the Governor. He's got the evidence of a woman ... Anyway, we'll hear it later."

'Now, I'm not much of a hand at describing mental states, so I can't tell you exactly what we felt then. Most of all was a fever and horror for fear they had already whisked Fred out and strung him up. But when we looked down into the yard from the Bridge of Sighs we saw Ed Nabors and the carpenter arguing over a cross-cut saw on the trap itself; and the blessed morning light coming up in glory to show us we could knock that ugly contraption to pieces and burn it.

'The corridor downstairs was deserted. Judge Hunt had got his wind back, and, being one of those stern elocutionists who like to make complimentary remarks about God, he was going on something powerful. He sobered up when he saw that the door to Fred Joliffe's cell was open.

' "Even Joliffe," says the judge, "deserves to get this news first."

'But Fred never did get that news, unless his ghost was listening. I told you he was very small and light. His heels were a good eighteen inches off the floor as he hung by the neck from an iron peg in the wall of the cell. He was hanging from a noose made in a child's skipping-rope; black-faced dead already, with the whites of his eyes showing in slits, and his heels swinging over a kicked-away stool.

'No, son, we didn't think it was suicide for long. For a little while we were stunned, half crazy, naturally. It was like thinking about your troubles at three o'clock in the morning.

'But, you see, Fred's hands were still tied behind him. There was a bump on the back of his head, from a hammer that lay beside the stool. Somebody had walked in there with the hammer concealed behind his back, had stunned Fred when he wasn't looking, had run a slip-knot in that skipping-rope, and jerked him up a-flapping to strangle there. It was the creepiest part of the business, when we'd got that through our heads, and we all began loudly to tell each other where we'd been during the confusion. Nobody had noticed much. I was scared green.

'When we gathered round the table in Bob's office, Judge Hunt took hold of his nerve with both hands. He looked at Bob Moran, at Ed Nabors, at Doc Macdonald, and at me. One of us was the other hangman.

' "This is a bad business, gentlemen," says he, clearing his throat a couple of times like a nervous orator before he starts. "What I want to know is, who under sanity would strangle a man when he thought we intended to do it anyway, on a gallows?"

'Then Doc Macdonald turned nasty. "Well," says he, "if it comes to that, you might inquire where that skipping-rope came from to begin with."

' "I don't get you," says Bob Moran, bewildered-like.

' "Oh, don't you?" says Doc, and sticks out his whiskers. "Well, then, who was so dead set on this execution going through as scheduled that he wanted to use a gun when the trap wouldn't drop?"

'Bob made a noise as though he'd been hit in the stomach. He stood looking at Doc for a minute, with his hands hanging down – and then he went for him. He had Doc back across the table, banging his head on the edge, when people began to crowd into the room at the yells. Funny, too; the first one in was the jail carpenter, who was pretty sore at not being told that the hanging had been called off.

' "What do you want to start fighting for?" he says, fretful-like. He was bigger than Bob, and had him off Doc with a couple of heaves. "Why didn't you tell me what was going on? They say there ain't going to be any hanging. Is that right?"

'Judge Hunt nodded, and the carpenter – Barney Hicks, that's who it was; I remember now – Barney Hicks looked pretty peevish, and says:

' "All right, all right, but you hadn't ought to fight all over the joint like that." Then he looks at Ed Nabors. "What I want is my hammer. Where's my hammer, Ed? I been looking all over the place for it. What did you do with it?"

'Ed Nabors sits up, pours himself four fingers of rye, and swallows it.

' "Beg pardon, Barney," says he in the coolest voice I ever heard. "I must have left it in the cell," he says, "when I killed Fred Joliffe."

'Talk about silences! It was like one of those silences when the magician at the Opera House fires a gun and six doves fly out of an empty box. I couldn't believe it. But I remember Ed Nabors sitting big in the corner by the barred window, in his shiny black coat and string tie. His hands were on his knees, and he was looking from one to the other of us, smiling a little. He looked as old as the prophets then; and he'd got enough liquor to keep the nerve from twitching beside his eye. So he just sat there, very quietly, shifting the plug of tobacco around in his cheek, and smiling.

' "Judge," he says in a reflective way, "you got a call from the Governor at Harrisburg, didn't you? Uh-huh. I knew what it would be. A woman had come forward, hadn't she, to confess Fred Joliffe was innocent and she had killed Randall Fraser? Uh-huh. The woman was my daughter. Jessie couldn't face telling it here, you see. That was why she ran away from me and went to the Governor. She'd have kept quiet if you hadn't convicted Fred."

' "But why ... " shouts the judge. "*Why* ... '

' "It was like this," Ed goes on in that slow way of his. "She'd been on pretty intimate terms with Randall Fraser, Jessie had. And both Randall and Fred were having a whooping lot of fun threatening to tell the whole town about it. She was pretty near crazy, I think. And, you see, on the night of the murder Fred Joliffe was too drunk to remember anything that happened. He thought he *had* killed Randall, I suppose, when he woke up and found Randall dead and blood on his hands.

' "It's all got to come out now, I suppose," says he, nodding. "What did happen was that the three of 'em were in that back room, which Fred didn't remember. He and Randall had a fight while they were baiting Jessie; Fred whacked him hard enough with that mallet to lay him out, but all the blood he got was from a big splash over Randall's eye. Jessie ... Well,

Jessie finished the job when Fred ran away, that's all."

' "But, you damned fool," cries Bob Moran, and begins to pound the table, "why did you have to go and kill Fred when Jessie had confessed?"

' "You fellows wouldn't have convicted Jessie, would you?" says Ed, blinking round at us. "No. But, if Fred had lived after her confession, you'd have *had* to, boys. That was how I figured it out. Once Fred learned what did happen, that he wasn't guilty and she was, he'd never have let up until he'd carried that case to the Superior Court out of your hands. He'd have screamed all over the State until they either had to hang her or send her up for life. I couldn't stand that. As I say, that was how I figured it out, although my brain's not so clear these days. So," says he, nodding and leaning over to take aim at the cuspidor, "when I heard about that telephone call, I went into Fred's cell and finished *my* job."

' "But don't you understand," says Judge Hunt, in the way you'd reason with a lunatic, "that Bob Moran will have to arrest you for murder, and – "

'It was the peacefulness of Ed's expression that scared us then. He got up from his chair, and dusted his shiny black coat, and smiled at us.

' "Oh no," says he very clearly. "That's what you don't understand. You can't do a single damned thing to me. You can't even arrest me."

' "He's bughouse," says Bob Moran.

' "Am I?" says Ed affably. "Listen to me. I've committed what you might call a perfect murder, because I've done it legally ... Judge, what time did you talk to the Governor's office, and get the order for the execution to be called off? Be careful now."

'And I said, with the whole idea of the business suddenly hitting me:

' "It was maybe five minutes past nine, wasn't it, Judge? I remember the court-house clock striking when we were going over the Bridge of Sighs."

' "I remember it too," says Ed Nabors. "And Doc Macdonald will tell you that Fred Joliffe was dead before ever that clock struck nine. I have in my pocket," says he, unbuttoning his coat, "a court order which authorizes me to kill Fred Joliffe, by means of hanging by the neck – which I did – between the hours of eight and nine in the morning – which I also did. And I did it in full legal style before the order was countermanded. Well?"

'Judge Hunt took off his stovepipe hat and wiped his face with a bandana. We all looked at him.

' "You can't get away with this," says the judge, and grabs the sheriff's order off the table. "You can't trifle with the law in that way. And you can't execute sentence alone. Look here! 'In the presence of a qualified medical practitioner.' What do you say to that?"

' "Well, I can produce my medical diploma," says Ed, nodding again. "I may be a booze-hister, and mighty unreliable, but they haven't struck me off the register yet ... You lawyers are hell on the wording of the law," says he admiringly, "and it's the wording that's done for you this time. Until you get the law altered with some fancy words, there's nothing in that document to say that the doctor and the hangman can't be the same person."

'After a while Bob Moran turned round to the judge with a funny expression on his face. It might have been a grin.

' "This ain't according to morals," says he. "A fine citizen like Fred shouldn't get murdered like that. It's awful. Something's got to be done about it. As you said yourself this morning, Judge, he ought to have the law and nothing but the law. Is Ed right, Judge?"

' "Frankly, I don't know," says Judge Hunt, wiping his face again. "But, so far as I know, he is. What are you doing, Robert?"

' "I'm writing him out a cheque for fifty dollars," says Bob Moran, surprised-like. "We got to have it all nice and legal, haven't we?" '

XI

A Haunted Island

Algernon Blackwood

Towards the end of the war years, another broadcaster with deep, sombre tones became a favourite with listeners and enjoyed a lasting success which continued until his death in the early 1950's. He was known as 'The Ghost Man' and chilled his audiences with tales of the supernatural – many of them based on personal experience. Behind this persona *was Algernon Blackwood (1869-1951), the footloose son of Sir Stevenson Blackwood, who rebelled against his strict upbringing and became a world traveller. From these trips came the raw material which he later utilised in his extensive output of strange and mysterious tales. Blackwood began writing just before the turn of the century, and was already building quite a reputation when he got his first taste of broadcasting through his association with the series* Nightmares *in the 1930's. His natural ability as a storyteller plus his atmospheric voice, made him a natural for the radio, and it was only a matter of time before he was invited to host a regular series of programmes. These he continued to the time of his death, often writing as well as recounting the stories. The localities of these tales reflected his own wanderings: from the heart of Europe to the centre of big American cities, and from sedate English towns to the wilds of Canada. One of the most effective of his broadcasts was 'A Haunted Island' based on an eerie experience he had while living in Canada. In introducing the story, he remarked, 'The island of my tale was in the Muskoka Lakes of north Toronto and there I lived* alone *for a month one autumn. As soon as the summer visitors had left, Red Indians began to flit to and fro and there was strangeness in the air ... ' Just* how *strange, I shall leave you to discover for yourself.*

The following events occurred on a small island of isolated position in a large Canadian lake, to whose cool waters the

139

inhabitants of Montreal and Toronto flee for rest and recreation in the hot months. It is only to be regretted that events of such peculiar interest to the genuine student of the psychical should be entirely uncorroborated. Such unfortunately, however, is the case.

Our own party of nearly twenty had returned to Montreal that very day, and I was left in solitary possession for a week or two longer, in order to accomplish some important 'reading' for the law which I had foolishly neglected during the summer.

It was late in September, and the big trout and maskinonge were stirring themselves in the depths of the lake, and beginning slowly to move up to the surface waters as the north winds and early frosts lowered their temperature. Already the maples were crimson and gold, and the wild laughter of the loons echoed in sheltered bays that never knew their strange cry in the summer.

With a whole island to oneself, a two-storey cottage, a canoe, and only the chipmunks, and the farmer's weekly visit with eggs and bread, to disturb one, the opportunities for hard reading might be very great. It all depends!

The rest of the party had gone off with many warnings to beware of Indians, and not to stay late enough to be the victim of a frost that thinks nothing of forty below zero. After they had gone, the loneliness of the situation made itself unpleasantly felt. There were no other islands within six or seven miles, and though the mainland forests lay a couple of miles behind me, they stretched for a very great distance unbroken by any signs of human habitation. But, though the island was completely deserted and silent, the rocks and trees that had echoed human laughter and voices almost every hour of the day for two months could not fail to retain some memories of it all; and I was not surprised to fancy I heard a shout or a cry as I passed from rock to rock, and more than once to imagine that I heard my own name called aloud.

In the cottage there were six tiny bedrooms divided from one another by plain unvarnished partitions of pine. A wooden bedstead, a mattress, and a chair, stood in each room, but I only found two mirrors, and one of these was broken.

The boards creaked a good deal as I moved about, and the signs of occupation were so recent that I could hardly believe that I was alone. I half expected to find someone left behind, still trying to crowd into a box more than it would hold. The door of one room was stiff, and refused for a moment to open, and it required very little persuasion to imagine someone was holding the handle on the inside, and that when it opened I should meet a pair of human eyes.

A thorough search of the floor led me to select as my own sleeping quarters a little room with a diminutive balcony over the verandah roof. The room was very small, but the bed was large, and had the best mattress of them all. It was situated directly over the sitting-room where I should live and do my 'reading', and the miniature window looked out to the rising sun. With the exception of a narrow path which led from the front door and verandah through the trees to the boat-landing, the island was densely covered with maples, hemlocks, and cedars. The trees gathered in round the cottage so closely that the slightest wind made the branches scrape the roof and tap the wooden walls. A few moments after sunset the darkness became impenetrable, and ten yards beyond the glare of the lamps that shone through the sitting-room windows – of which there were four – you could not see an inch before your nose, nor move a step without running up against a tree.

The rest of that day I spent moving my belongings from my tent to the sitting-room, taking stock of the contents of the larder, and chopping enough wood for the stove to last me for a week. After that, just before sunset, I went round the island a couple of times in my canoe for precaution's sake. I had never dreamed of doing this before, but when a man is alone he does things that never occur to him when he is one of a large party.

How lonely the island seemed when I landed again! The sun was down, and twilight is unknown in these northern regions. The darkness comes up at once. The canoe safely pulled up and turned over on her face, I groped my way up the little narrow pathway to the verandah. The six lamps were soon burning merrily in the front room; but in the kitchen, where I 'dined', the shadows were so gloomy, and the lamplight was so inadequate, that the stars could be seen peeping through the cracks between the rafters.

I turned in early that night. Though it was calm and there was no wind, the creaking of my bedstead and the musical gurgle of the water over the rocks below were not the only sounds that reached my ears. As I lay awake, the appalling emptiness of the house grew upon me. The corridors and vacant rooms seemed to echo innumerable footsteps, shufflings, the rustle of skirts, and a constant undertone of whispering. When sleep at length overtook me, the breathings and noises, however, passed gently to mingle with the voices of my dreams.

A week passed by, and the 'reading' progressed favourably. On the tenth day of my solitude, a strange thing happened. I awoke after a good night's sleep to find myself possessed with a marked repugnance for my room. The air seemed to stifle me. The more I tried to define the cause of this dislike, the more unreasonable it appeared. There was something about the room that made me afraid. Absurd as it seems, this feeling clung to me obstinately while dressing, and more than once I caught myself shivering, and conscious of an inclination to get out of the room as quickly as possible. The more I tried to laugh it away, the more real it became; and when at last I was dressed, and went out into the passage, and downstairs into the kitchen, it was with feelings of relief, such as I might imagine would accompany one's escape from the presence of a dangerous contagious disease.

While cooking my breakfast, I carefully recalled every night spent in the room, in the hope that I might in some way connect the dislike I now felt with some disagreeable incident that had occurred in it. But the only thing I could recall was one stormy night when I suddenly awoke and heard the boards creaking so loudly in the corridor that I was convinced there were people in the house. So certain was I of this, that I had descended the stairs, gun in hand, only to find the doors and windows securely fastened, and the mice and black-beetles in sole possession of the floor. This was certainly not sufficient to account for the strength of my feelings.

The morning hours I spent in steady reading; and when I broke off in the middle of the day for a swim and luncheon, I was very much surprised, if not a little alarmed, to find that my dislike for the room had, if anything, grown stronger. Going upstairs to get a book, I experienced the most marked aversion to entering the room, and while within I was conscious all the time of an uncomfortable feeling that was half uneasiness and half apprehension. The result of it was that, instead of reading, I spent the afternoon on the water paddling and fishing, and when I got home about sundown, brought with me half a dozen delicious black bass for the supper-table and the larder.

As sleep was an important matter to me at this time, I had decided that if my aversion to the room was so strongly marked on my return as it had been before, I would move my bed down into the sitting-room, and sleep there. This was, I argued, in no sense a concession to an absurd and fanciful fear, but simply a precaution to ensure a good night's sleep. A bad night involved the loss of the next day's reading, – a loss I was not prepared to incur.

I accordingly moved my bed downstairs into a corner of the sitting-room facing the door, and was moreover uncommonly glad when the operation was completed, and the door of the bedroom closed finally upon the shadows, the silence, and the strange *fear* that shared the room with them.

The croaking stroke of the kitchen clock sounded the hour of eight as I finished washing up my few dishes, and closing the kitchen door behind me, passed into the front room. All the lamps were lit, and their reflectors, which I had polished up during the day, threw a blaze of light into the room.

Outside the night was still and warm. Not a breath of air was stirring; the waves were silent, the trees motionless, and heavy clouds hung like an oppressive curtain over the heavens. The darkness seemed to have rolled up with unusual swiftness, and not the faintest glow of colour remained to show where the sun had set. There was present in the atmosphere that ominous and overwhelming silence which so often precedes the most violent storms.

I sat down to my books with my brain unusually clear, and in my heart the pleasant satisfaction of knowing that five black bass were lying in the ice-house, and that tomorrow morning the old farmer would arrive with fresh bread and eggs. I was soon absorbed in my books.

As the night wore on the silence deepened. Even the chipmunks were still; and the boards of the floors and walls ceased creaking. I read on steadily till, from the gloomy shadows of the kitchen, came the hoarse sound of the clock striking nine. How loud the strokes sounded! They were like blows of a big hammer. I closed one book and opened another, feeling that I was just warming up to my work.

This, however, did not last long. I presently found that I was reading the same paragraphs over twice, simple paragraphs that did not require such effort. Then I noticed that my mind began to wander to other things, and the effort to recall my thoughts became harder with each digression. Concentration was growing momentarily more difficult. Presently I discovered that I had turned over two pages instead of one, and had not noticed my mistake until I was well down the page. This was becoming serious. What was the disturbing influence? It could not be physical fatigue. On the contrary, my mind was unusually alert, and in a more receptive condition than usual. I made a new and determined effort to read, and for a short time succeeded in giving my whole attention to my subject. But in a very few moments again I found myself leaning back in my chair, staring vacantly into space.

Something was evidently at work in my subconsciousness. There was something I had neglected to do. Perhaps the kitchen door and windows were not fastened. I accordingly went to see, and found that they were! The fire perhaps needed attention. I went to see, and found that it was all right! I looked at the lamps, went upstairs into every bedroom in turn, and then went round the house, and even into the ice-house. Nothing was wrong; everything was in its place. Yet something *was* wrong! The conviction grew stronger and stronger within me.

When I at length settled down to my books again and tried to read, I became aware, for the first time, that the room seemed growing cold. Yet the day had been oppressively warm, and evening had brought no relief. The six big lamps, moreover, gave out heat enough to warm the room pleasantly. But a chilliness, that perhaps crept up from the lake, made itself felt in the room, and caused me to get up to close the glass door opening on to the verandah.

For a brief moment I stood looking out at the shaft of light that fell from the windows and shone some little distance down the pathway, and out for a few feet into the lake.

As I looked, I saw a canoe glide into the pathway of light, and immediately crossing it, pass out of sight again into the darkness. It was perhaps a hundred feet from the shore, and it moved swiftly.

I was surprised that a canoe should pass the island at that time of night, for all the summer visitors from the other side of the lake had gone home weeks before, and the island was a long way out of any line of water traffic.

My reading from this moment did not make very good progress, for somehow the picture of that canoe, gliding so dimly and swiftly across the narrow track of light on the black waters, silhouetted itself against the background of my mind with singular vividness. It kept coming between my eyes and the printed page. The more I thought about it the more surprised I became. It was of larger build than any I had seen during the past summer months, and was more like the old Indian war canoes with the high curving bows and stern and wide beam. The more I tried to read, the less success attended my efforts; and finally I closed my books and went out on the verandah to walk up and down a bit, and shake the chilliness out of my bones.

The night was perfectly still, and as dark as imaginable. I stumbled down the path to the little landing wharf, where the water made the very faintest of gurgling under the timbers. The sound of a big tree falling in the mainland forest, far across the lake, stirred echoes in the heavy air, like the first guns of a distant night attack. No other sound disturbed the stillness that reigned supreme.

As I stood upon the wharf in the broad splash of light that followed me from the sitting-room windows, I saw another canoe cross the pathway of uncertain light upon the water, and disappear at once into the impenetrable gloom that lay beyond. This time I saw more distinctly than before. It was like the former canoe, a big birch-bark, with high-crested bows and stern and broad beam. It was paddled by two Indians, of whom the one in the stern – the steerer – appeared to be a very large man. I could see this very plainly; and though the second canoe was much nearer the island than the first, I judged that they were both on their way home to the Government Reservation, which was situated some fifteen miles away upon the mainland.

I was wondering in my mind what could possibly bring any Indians down to this part of the lake at such an hour of the night, when a third canoe, of precisely similar build, and also occupied by two Indians, passed silently round the end of the wharf. This time the canoe was very much nearer shore, and it suddenly flashed into my mind that the three canoes were in reality one and the same, and that only one canoe was circling the island!

This was by no means a pleasant reflection, because, if it were the correct solution of the unusual appearance of the three canoes in this lonely part of the lake at so late an hour, the purpose of the two men could only reasonably be considered to be in some way connected with myself. I had never known of the Indians attempting any violence upon the settlers who shared the wild, inhospitable country with them; at the same time, it was not beyond the region of possibility to suppose ... But then I did not care even to think of such hideous possibilities, and my imagination immediately sought relief in all manner of other solutions to the problem, which indeed came readily enough to my mind, but did not succeed in recommending themselves to my reason.

Meanwhile, by a sort of instinct, I stepped back out of the bright light in which I had hitherto been standing, and waited in the deep shadow of a rock to see if the canoe would again make its appearance. Here I could see, without being seen, and the precaution seemed a wise one.

After less than five minutes the canoe, as I had anticipated, made its fourth appearance. This time it was not twenty yards from the wharf, and I saw that the Indians meant to land. I recognized the two men as those who had passed before, and the steerer was certainly an immense fellow. It was unquestionably the same canoe. There could be no longer any doubt that for some purpose of their own the men had been going round and round the island for some time, waiting for an opportunity to land. I strained my eyes to follow them in the darkness, but the night had completely swallowed them up, and not even the faintest swish of paddles reached my ears as the Indians plied their long and powerful strokes. The canoe would be round again in a few minutes, and this time it was possible that the men might land. It was well to be prepared. I

knew nothing of their intentions, and two to one (when the two
are big Indians!) late at night on a lonely island was not exactly
my idea of pleasant intercourse.

In a corner of the sitting-room, leaning up against the back
wall, stood my Marlin rifle, with ten cartridges in the magazine
and one lying snugly in the greased breech. There was just time
to get up to the house and take up a position of defence in that
corner. Without an instant's hesitation I ran up to the
verandah, carefully picking my way among the trees, so as to
avoid being seen in the light. Entering the room, I shut the
door leading to the verandah, and as quickly as possible turned
out every one of the six lamps. To be in a room so brilliantly
lighted, where my every movement could be observed from
outside, while I could see nothing but impenetrable darkness
at every window, was by all laws of warfare an unnecessary
concession to the enemy. And this enemy, if enemy it was to be,
was far too wily and dangerous to be granted any such
advantages.

I stood in the corner of the room with my back against the
wall, and my hand on the cold rifle-barrel. The table, covered
with my books, lay between me and the door, but for the first
few minutes after the lights were out the darkness was so
intense that nothing could be discerned at all. Then, very
gradually, the outline of the room became visible, and the
framework of the windows began to shape itself dimly before
my eyes.

After a few minutes the door (its upper half of glass), and the
two windows that looked out upon the front verandah, became
specially distinct; and I was glad that this was so, because if the
Indians came up to the house I should be able to see their
approach, and gather something of their plans. Nor was I
mistaken, for there presently came to my ears the peculiar
hollow sound of a canoe landing and being carefully dragged
up over the rocks. The paddles I distinctly heard being placed
underneath, and the silence that ensued thereupon I rightly
interpreted to mean that the Indians were stealthily
approaching the house ...

While it would be absurd to claim that I was not alarmed –
even frightened – at the gravity of the situation and its possible
outcome, I speak the whole truth when I say that I was not

overwhelmingly afraid for myself. I was conscious that even at this stage of the night I was passing into a psychical condition in which my sensations seemed no longer normal. Physical fear at no time entered into the nature of my feelings; and though I kept my hand upon my rifle the greater part of the night, I was all the time conscious that its assistance could be of little avail against the terrors that I had to face. More than once I seemed to feel most curiously that I was in no real sense a part of the proceedings, nor actually involved in them, but that I was playing the part of a spectator – a spectator, moreover, on a psychic rather than on a material plane. Many of my sensations that night were too vague for definite description and analysis, but the main feeling that will stay with me to the end of my days is the awful horror of it all, and the miserable sensation that if the strain had lasted a little longer than was actually the case my mind must inevitably have given way.

Meanwhile I stood still in my corner, and waited patiently for what was to come. The house was as still as the grave, but the inarticulate voices of the night sang in my ears, and I seemed to hear the blood running in my veins and dancing in my pulses.

If the Indians came to the back of the house, they would find the kitchen door and window securely fastened. They could not get in there without making considerable noise, which I was bound to hear. The only mode of getting in was by means of the door that faced me, and I kept my eyes glued on that door without taking them off for the smallest fraction of a second.

My sight adapted itself every minute better to the darkness. I saw the table that nearly filled the room, and left only a narrow passage on each side. I could also make out the straight backs of the wooden chairs pressed up against it, and could even distinguish my papers and inkstand lying on the white oilcloth covering. I thought of the gay faces that had gathered round that table during the summer, and I longed for the sunlight as I had never longed for it before.

Less than three feet to my left the passage-way led to the kitchen, and the stairs leading to the bedrooms above commenced in this passage-way, but almost in the sitting-room itself. Through the windows I could see the dim motionless outlines of the trees: not a leaf stirred, not a branch moved.

A few moments of this awful silence, and then I was aware of a

soft tread on the boards of the verandah, so stealthy that it
seemed an impression directly on my brain rather than upon
the nerves of hearing. Immediately afterwards a black figure
darkened the glass door, and I perceived that a face was
pressed against the upper panes. A shiver ran down my back,
and my hair was conscious of a tendency to rise and stand at
right angles to my head.

It was the figure of an Indian, broad-shouldered and
immense; indeed, the largest figure of a man I have ever seen
outside of a circus hall. By some power of light that seemed to
generate itself in the brain, I saw the strong dark face with the
aquiline nose and high cheek-bones flattened against the glass.
The direction of the gaze I could not determine; but faint
gleams of light as the big eyes rolled round and showed their
whites, told me plainly that no corner of the room escaped
their searching.

For what seemed fully five minutes the dark figure stood
there, with the huge shoulders bent forward so as to bring the
head down to the level of the glass; while behind him, though
not nearly so large, the shadowy form of the other Indian
swayed to and fro like a bent tree. While I waited in an agony
of suspense and agitiation for their next movement little
currents of icy sensation ran up and down my spine and my
heart seemed alternately to stop beating and then start off
again with terrifying rapidity. They must have heard its
thumping and the singing of the blood in my head! Moreover,
I was conscious, as I felt a cold stream of perspiration trickle
down my face, of a desire to scream, to shout, to bang the walls
like a child, to make a noise, or do anything that would relieve
the suspense and bring things to a speedy climax.

It was probably this inclination that led me to another
discovery, for when I tried to bring my rifle from behind my
back to raise it and have it pointed at the door ready to fire, I
found that I was powerless to move. The muscles, paralysed by
this strange fear, refused to obey the will. Here indeed was a
terrifying complication!

*

There was a faint sound of rattling at the brass knob, and the
door was pushed open a couple of inches. A pause of a few

seconds, and it was pushed open still further. Without a sound of footsteps that was appreciable to my ears, the two figures glided into the room, and the man behind gently closed the door after him.

They were alone with me between the four walls. Could they see me standing there, so still and straight in my corner? Had they, perhaps, already seen me? My blood surged and sang like the roll of drums in an orchestra; and though I did my best to suppress my breathing, it sounded like the rushing of wind through a pneumatic tube.

My suspense as to the next move was soon at an end – only, however, to give place to a new and keener alarm. The men had hitherto exchanged no words and no signs, but there were general indications of a movement across the room, and whichever way they went they would have to pass round the table. If they came my way they would have to pass within six inches of my person. While I was considering this very disagreeable possibility, I perceived that the smaller Indian (smaller by comparison) suddenly raised his arm and pointed to the ceiling. The other fellow raised his head and followed the direction of his companion's arm. I began to understand at last. They were going upstairs, and the room directly overhead to which they pointed had been until this night my bedroom. It was the room in which I had experienced that very morning so strange a sensation of fear, and but for which I should then have been lying asleep in the narrow bed against the window.

The Indians then began to move silently around the room; they were going upstairs, and they were coming round my side of the table. So stealthy were their movements that, but for the abnormally sensitive state of the nerves, I should never have heard them. As it was, their cat-like tread was distinctly audible. Like two monstrous black cats they came round the table toward me, and for the first time I perceived that the smaller of the two dragged something along the floor behind him. As it trailed along over the floor with a soft, sweeping sound, I somehow got the impression that it was a large dead thing with outstretched wings, or a large, spreading cedar branch. Whatever it was, I was unable to see it even in outline, and I was too terrified, even had I possessed the power over my muscles, to move my head forward in the effort to determine its nature.

Nearer and nearer they came. The leader rested a giant hand upon the table as he moved. My lips were glued together, and the air seemed to burn in my nostrils. I tried to close my eyes, so that I might not see as they passed me; but my eyelids had stiffened, and refused to obey. Would they never get by me? Sensation seemed also to have left my legs, and it was as if I were standing on mere supports of wood or stone. Worse still, I was conscious that I was losing the power of balance, the power to stand upright, or even to lean backwards against the wall. Some force was drawing me forward, and a dizzy terror seized me that I should lose my balance, and topple forward against the Indians just as they were in the act of passing me.

Even moments drawn out into hours must come to an end some time, and almost before I knew it the figures had passed me and had their feet upon the lower step of the stairs leading to the upper bedrooms. There could not have been six inches between us, and yet I was conscious only of a current of cold air that followed them. They had not touched me, and I was convinced that they had not seen me. Even the trailing thing on the floor behind them had not touched my feet, as I had dreaded it would, and on such an occasion as this I was grateful even for the smallest mercies.

The absence of the Indians from my immediate neighbourhood brought little sense of relief. I stood shivering and shuddering in my corner, and, beyond being able to breathe more freely, I felt no whit less uncomfortable. Also, I was aware that a certain light, which, without apparent source or rays, had enabled me to follow their every gesture and movement, had gone out of the room with their departure. An unnatural darkness now filled the room, and pervaded its every corner so that I could barely make out the positions of the windows and the glass doors.

As I said before, my condition was evidently an abnormal one. The capacity for feeling surprise seemed, as in dreams, to be wholly absent. My senses recorded with unusual accuracy every smallest occurrence, but I was able to draw only the simplest deductions.

The Indians soon reached the top of the stairs, and there they halted for a moment. I had not the faintest clue as to their next movement. They appeared to hesitate. They were listening attentively. Then I heard one of them, who by the weight of his soft tread must have been the giant, cross the narrow corridor and enter the room directly overhead – my own little bedroom. But for the insistence of that unaccountable dread I had experienced there in the morning, I should at that very moment have been lying in the bed with the big Indian in the room standing beside me.

For the space of a hundred seconds there was silence, such as might have existed before the birth of sound. It was followed by a long quivering shriek of terror, which rang out into the night, and ended in a short gulp before it had run its full course. At the same moment the other Indian left his place at the head of the stairs, and joined his companion in the bedroom. I heard the 'thing' trailing behind him along the floor. A thud followed, as of something heavy falling, and then all became as still and silent as before.

It was at this point that the atmosphere, surcharged all day with the electricity of a fierce storm, found relief in a dancing flash of brilliant lightning simultaneously with a crash of loudest thunder. For five seconds every article in the room was visible to me with amazing distinctness, and through the windows I saw the tree trunks standing in solemn rows. The thunder pealed and echoed across the lake and among the distant islands, and the flood-gates of heaven then opened and let out their rain in streaming torrents.

The drops fell with a swift rushing sound upon the still waters of the lake, which leaped up to meet them, and pattered with the rattle of shot on the leaves of the maples and the roof of the cottage. A moment later, and another flash, even more brilliant and of longer duration than the first, lit up the sky from zenith to horizon, and bathed the room momentarily in dazzling whiteness. I could see the rain glistening on the leaves and branches outside. The wind rose suddenly, and in less than a minute the storm that had been gathering all day burst forth in its full fury.

Above all the noisy voices of the elements, the slightest sounds in the room overhead made themselves heard, and in the few seconds of deep silence that followed the shriek of terror and pain I was aware that the movements had commenced again. The men were leaving the room and approaching the top of the stairs. A short pause, and they began to descend. Behind them, tumbling from step to step, I could hear that trailing 'thing' being dragged along. It had become ponderous!

I awaited their approach with a degree of calmness, almost of apathy, which was only explicable on the ground that after a certain point Nature applies her own anaesthetic, and a merciful condition of numbness supervenes. On they came, step by step, nearer and nearer, with the shuffling sound of the burden behind growing louder as they approached.

They were already half-way down the stairs when I was galvanized afresh into a condition of terror by the consideration of a new and horrible possibility. It was the reflection that if another vivid flash of lightning were to come when the shadowy procession was in the room, perhaps when it was actually passing in front of me, I should see everything in detail, and worse, be seen myself! I could only hold my breath and wait – wait while the minutes lengthened into hours, and the procession made its slow progress round the room.

The Indians had reached the foot of the staircase. The form of the huge leader loomed in the doorway of the passage, and the burden with an ominous thud had dropped from the last step to the floor. There was a moment's pause while I saw the Indian turn and stoop to assist his companion. Then the procession moved forward again, entered the room close on my left, and began to move slowly round my side of the table. The leader was already beyond me, and his companion, dragging on the floor behind him the burden, whose confused outline I could dimly make out, was exactly in front of me, when the cavalcade came to a dead halt. At the same moment, with the strange suddenness of thunderstorms, the splash of the rain ceased altogether, and the wind died away into utter silence.

For the space of five seconds my heart seemed to stop beating, and then the worst came. A double flash of lightning lit up the room and its contents with merciless vividness.

The huge Indian leader stood a few feet past me on my right. One leg was stretched forward in the act of taking a step. His immense shoulders were turned towards his companion, and in all their magnificent fierceness I saw the outline of his features. His gaze was directed upon the burden his companion was dragging along the floor; but his profile, with the big aquiline nose, high cheek-bone, straight black hair and bold chin, burnt itself in that brief instant into my brain, never again to fade.

Dwarfish, compared with this gigantic figure, appeared the proportions of the other Indian, who, within twelve inches of my face, was stooping over the thing he was dragging in a position that lent to his person the additional horror of deformity. And the burden, lying upon a sweeping cedar branch which he held and dragged by a long stem, was the body of a white man. The scalp had been neatly lifted, and blood lay in a broad smear upon the cheeks and forehead.

Then, for the first time that night, the terror that had paralysed my muscles and my will will lifted its unholy spell from my soul. With a loud cry I stretched out my arms to seize the big Indian by the throat, and, grasping only air, tumbled forward unconscious upon the ground.

I had recognized the body, and *the face was my own!* ...

It was bright daylight when a man's voice recalled me to consciousness. I was lying where I had fallen, and the farmer was standing in the room with the loaves of bread in his hands. The horror of the night was still in my heart, and as the bluff settler helped me to my feet and picked up the rifle which had fallen with me, with many questions and expressions of condolence, I imagined my brief replies were neither self-exaplanatory nor even intelligible.

That day, after a thorough and fruitless search of the house, I left the island, and went over to spend my last ten days with the farmer; and when the time came for me to leave, the necessary reading had been accomplished, and my nerves had completely recovered their balance.

On the day of my departure the farmer started early in his big boat with my belongings to row to the point, twelve miles distant, where a little steamer ran twice a week for the accommodation of hunters. Late in the afternoon I went off in another direction in my canoe, wishing to see the island once again, where I had been the victim of so strange an experience.

In due course I arrived there, and made a tour of the island. I also made a search of the little house, and it was not without a curious sensation in my heart that I entered the little upstairs bedroom. There seemed nothing unusual.

Just after I re-embarked, I saw a canoe gliding ahead of me around the curve of the island. A canoe was an unusual sight at this time of the year, and this one seemed to have sprung from nowhere. Altering my course a little, I watched it disappear around the next projecting point of rock. It had high curving bows, and there were two Indians in it. I lingered with some excitement, to see if it would appear again round the other side of the island; and in less than five minutes it came into view. There were less than two hundred yards between us, and the Indians, sitting on their haunches, were paddling swiftly in my direction.

I never paddled faster in my life than I did in those next few minutes. When I turned to look again, the Indians had altered their course, and were again circling the island.

The sun was sinking behind the forests on the mainland, and the crimson-coloured clouds of sunset were reflected in the waters of the lake, when I looked round for the last time, and saw the big bark canoe and its two dusky occupants still going round the island. Then the shadows deepened rapidly; the lake grew black, and the night wind blew its first breath in my face as I turned a corner, and a projecting bluff of rock hid from my view both island and canoe.

XII

The Golem

Gustav Meyrink

Although the world's first television service had been started as early as November 1936 in London, it was not until the 1950's that TV really surpassed radio in terms of popularity. Inevitably, of course, radio would never be able to regain its position of pre-eminence as a medium of home entertainment: but nonetheless it was still able to offer a special kind of entertainment which by its very nature allowed freer reign for the imagination than television. This said, it is no surprise to find that tales of the supernatural have continued to be a staple feature of broadcasting to this day. Two outstanding examples from either side of the Atlantic will suffice to show this and neatly round off the collection. In America, the most popular show of this kind has been CBS Radio's Mystery Theatre *masterminded by Himan Brown, of* Inner Sanctum *fame. For his work on that earlier show, Brown had earned a reputation as a 'genius of radio mystery' and he was a natural choice when CBS decided to revive this kind of weekly series in 1973. Once again, Brown made an inspired choice when he picked the veteran actor E.G.Marshall to host the show. The hour-long* Mystery Theatre *has since drawn on many of the classic ghost and horror stories for its productions, but has also sometimes updated and relocated them with striking effect. This, Himan Brown believes, has given the series greater impact with modern audiences surfeited with television. He has also constantly experimented with sound effects. 'We are always inventing monsters,' he says, 'because I have to give the monster substance. If he's a wraith, I have to make a wraith. If he's a ghost – what does a ghost sound like? So we're constantly playing around with electronic effects – and all that radio can give to make the total feeling much more monstrous.' The series has also featured such familiar actors as Ralph Bell, Howard DaSilva, Keir*

Dullea, Celeste Holm, and the Academy award winner Mercedes McCambridge, believed by many people (including Orson Welles) to be the greatest living radio actress. Arguably one of the most daunting challenges Himan Brown faced was putting the story of 'The Golem' by Gustav Meyrink (1868-1932) on the air in 1975. Meyrinks's classic story based on the Czechoslovakian legend of the man of clay who is brought to life by ancient magic featured a character at once monstrous and yet somehow pathetic, and the adaptation demanded the highest skills of production and effects as well as outstanding performances from the actors Ralph Bell, Larry Haines, Mandel Kramer and Mason Adams. Here, to represent American radio mystery at its recent best, is the macabre story of the Golem as narrated by a student of magical lore named Athanasius Pernath ...

There were four of us that night in my little room: Joshua Prokop, the musician; the old puppeteer, Zwakh; Vrieslander the artist, and myself. We had opened the window to try and let the smell of tobacco smoke out, and a cold wind now blew in, making the curtain that hung over the door sway to and fro.

'Prokop's worthy headgear would like to take unto itself wings and fly away,' said Zwakh, and pointed to the musician's hat, which was flapping its broad brim like black wings.

Joshua Prokop's eyes twinkled.

'It wants to go ... ' he said.

'It wants to go dancing at Loisitschek's,' Vrieslander finished for him.

Prokop laughed again, and started to beat time with one hand to the noises borne over the roof on the wings of the winter breeze. Then, from the wall, he took down my old guitar, and made as though he would pluck its broken strings, while he sang in his cracky falsetto, and with fantastic phrasing a remarkable song in dialect:

> *An Bein-del von Ei-sen recht alt*
> *An Stran-zen net gar a so kalt*
> *Messinung, a'Raucherl und Rohn*
> *Und immer nurr put-zen ...*

'He's a dab hand at the dialect all right, isn't he?' laughed Vrieslander.

'They sing that old song every evening down at Loisitschek's,' Zwakh informed me. 'The old fellow Nephtali Schaffraneck, with his green shade over his eyes, wheezes it out, accompanied on the accordion by a painted piece of female goods. Really, you know, Master Pernath, you ought to go along with us there some evening. Perhaps to-night – later – when we're through with the punch – eh? What do you say to it? Isn't it your birthday to-day, or something?'

'Yes,' urged Prokop, as he closed the window once more, 'You come along with us, old fellow-me-lad. It's a thing to see for yourself.'

We sat around drinking hot punch, while our thoughts roamed the room.

Vrieslander was carving a puppet.

'Well, Joshua,' – Zwakh broke the silence – 'you've shut us off good and proper from the outer world. Not one word has got itself spoken since you shut the window.'

'I was thinking,' said Prokop, rather hurriedly, as if apologising for his own silence, 'while the curtain was flapping, how odd it is when the wind plays with inanimate objects. It's almost like a miracle when things that lie about without a particle of life in their bodies suddenly start to flutter. Haven't you ever felt that? Once I stood in a desolate square and watched a whole heap of scraps of paper chasing one another. I couldn't feel the wind, as I was in the shelter of a house, but there they were, all chasing each other, murder in their hearts. Next instant they appeared to have decided on an armistice, but all of a sudden some unendurable puff of bitterness seemed to blow through the lot of them, and off they went again, each hounding on his next-door neighbour till they disappeared round the corner. One solid piece of newspaper only lagged behind; it lay helplessly on the pavement, flapping venomously up and down, like a fish out of water, gasping for air. I couldn't help the thought that rose in me: if we, when all's said and done, aren't something similar to these little bits of fluttering paper. Driven hither and thither by some invisible, incomprehensible "wind" that dictates all our actions, while we in our simplicity think we have free will. Supposing life really were nothing but that mysterious whirlwind of which the Bible states, it "bloweth where it listeth, and thou hearest the sound thereof, but canst not tell whence it cometh and whither it goeth"! Isn't there a dream in which we fumble in deep pools after silver fish, and catch them, to wake and find nothing in our hands but a cold draught of air blowing through them?'

'Prokop, you're catching that trick of speech from Pernath! What's the matter with you?' Zwakh regarded the musician suspiciously.

'It's the result of the story of the book *Ibbur* we had told to us before you came. Pity you were late and missed it … you can see the effect it's had on Prokop.' This from Vrieslander.

'Story about a book?'

'Story of a man, rather, who brought the book, and looked very strange. Pernath doesn't know who he is, where he lives, what his name is, or what he wanted. And, for all his visitor's striking appearance, he can't for the life of him describe it.'

Zwakh listened attentively.

'Strange, that,' he said, after a pause. 'Was the stranger clean shaven by any chance, and did his eyes slant?'

'I think so,' replied I. 'That is to say … yes … yes … I am quite sure of it. Do you know him?'

The puppeteer shook his head. 'Only it reminds me of the Golem.'

Vrieslander, the artist, laid down his knife.

'The Golem? I've heard of it a lot. Do you know anything about the Golem, Zwakh?'

'Who can say he *knows* anything about the Golem?' was Zwakh's rejoinder, as he shrugged his shoulders. 'Always they treat it as a legend, till something happens and turns it into actuality again. After which it's talked of for many a day. The rumours wax more and more fantastic, till the whole business gets so exaggerated and overdone that it dies of its own absurdity.

'The original story harks back, so they say, to the sixteenth century. Using long-lost formulas from the Kabbala, a rabbi is said to have made an artificial man – the so-called Golem – to help ring the bells in the Synagogue and for all kinds of other menial work.

'But he hadn't made a full man, and it was animated by a sort of vegetable half-life. What life it had, too, so the story runs, was only derived from a magic charm placed behind its teeth each day, that drew down to itself what was known as the "free sidereal strength of the universe."

'One evening, before evening prayers, the rabbi forgot to take the charm out of the Golem's mouth, and it fell into a frenzy. It raged through the dark streets, smashing everything in its path, until the rabbi caught up with it, removed the charm, and destroyed it. Then the Golem collapsed, lifeless. All that was left of it was a small clay image, which you can still see in the Old Synagogue.'

'The same rabbi was once summoned to the Imperial Palace by the Emperor, where he conjured up the spirits of the dead and made them visible,' put in Prokop. 'The modern theory is that he used a magic lantern.'

'Oh, yes,' said Zwakh composedly. 'That explanation is foolish enough to appeal to moderns. A magic lantern! As if Kaiser Rudolf, who spent his life chasing after such things, couldn't have spotted a blatant fraud like that at first glance.

'I don't know how the Golem story originated, but this I know – there is something here in this quarter of the town ... something that cannot die, and has its being within our midst. From generation to generation, my ancestors have lived in this place, and no one has heard more direct experiences and traditional stories than I have.'

Zwakh suddenly ceased speaking. It was obvious his thoughts had gone trailing off into the past.

As he sat there at the table, head on hand, his rosy, youthful-looking cheeks contrasting oddly in the lamplight with his snowy hair, I could hardly refrain from comparing his face with the little puppets he had so often shown to me. Curious how the old fellow resembled them! The same expression, and the same cast of countenance.

There are many things on earth that cannot be separated, I pondered. As Zwakh's simple life-history passed before my mind's eye, it struck me as both monstrous and weird that a man such as he, in spite of a better education than that of his forebears – he had, as a matter of fact, been destined for the stage – should suddenly insist on reverting to his dilapidated box of marionettes, trundling once more into the market-place these aged dolls that had anticked for the scanty living of his ancestors, and there making them re-enact their well-worn histories in terms of clumsy gesture.

I appreciated the reason. He could not endure to be parted from them; their lives were bound up with his, and once he was away from them they changed to thoughts within his brain, where they led him a restless existence till he returned to them. For that reason he did love them and trick them out proudly.

'Won't you tell us some more, Zwakh?' Prokop begged the old man, with a glance at myself and Vrieslander that sought approval.

'I hardly know where to begin,' the old man said hesitantly, 'Golem stories are all hard telling. Pernath, here, just now was telling us he knew quite well how the stranger looked, but couldn't describe him. More or less every three and thirty years something takes place in our streets, not so out-of-the-way or startling in itself, yet the terror of it is too strong for either explanation or excuse.

'Always it happens that an apparition makes its appearance – an utterly strange man, clean shaven, of yellow complexion, Mongolian type, in antiquated clothes of a bygone day; it comes from the direction of the Altschulgasse, stalks through the Ghetto with a queer groping, stumbling kind of gait, as if afraid of falling over, and quite suddenly – is gone.

'Usually it is seen to disappear round a corner. At other times it is said to have described a circle and gone back to the point whence it started – an old house, close by the Synagogue.

'Some people will tell how they have seen it coming towards them down a street, but, as they walked boldly to meet it, it would grow smaller and smaller, like an ordinary figure will do as it moves away from you, and finally disappear completely.

'Sixty-six years ago there must have been a particularly lively scare of this sort, for I remember – I was a tiny youngster at the time – that the house in the Altschulgasse was searched from top to bottom. It is also said that there is a room there with a barred window, but no entrance. They hung washing out of every window, and the room was discovered. As the only means of reaching it, a man let himself down on a rope from the roof, to see in. But no sooner did he get near the window than the rope broke and the poor fellow fractured his skull upon the pavement. And when they wanted, later on, to try again, opinions differed so about the situation of the window that they gave it up.

'I myself encountered the Golem for the first time in my life nearly three and thirty years ago. I met it in a little alley, and we ran right into one another. I still cannot remember now very distinctly what went on in my mind at that encounter. Heaven forbid anyone should spend his life in perpetual expectation, day in, day out, of meeting the Golem. At that moment, before I had seen anything, something cried out in me, loud and shrill, "The Golem!" At that instant someone stumbled out of a doorway and the strange figure passed me by. Next moment I was surrounded by a sea of white, frightened faces, everyone asking if I had seen it.

'As I replied, I was aware for the first time that my tongue had been released as from a clamp. I was quite surprised to find that I could move my limbs, for I realised how, for the space of a heart beat, I must have endured a sort of paralytic shock from surprise.

'I have given the subject much thought, and the nearest I can get to the truth of it seems to be this: that once in every generation a spiritual disturbance zigzags, like a flash of lightning, right through the Ghetto, taking possession of the souls of the living to some end we know not of, and rising in the form of a wraith that appears to our senses in the guise of a human entity that once, centuries ago, maybe, lived here, and is craving materialisation.

'Maybe, too, it lurks within our midst, day after day, and we know it not. Neither do our ears register the sound of the tuning-fork till it is brought in contact with the wood, which it forces into sympathetic vibration.

'Think of the crystal, resolving itself, it knows not how, but in accordance with its own immutable laws, from the formless, to a definite ordered shape. May it not be even so in the world of the spirit? Who shall say? Just as, in thundery weather, the electric tension in the atmosphere will increase to a point past endurance, and eventually give birth to the lightning, may it not be that the whole mass of stagnant thought infecting the air of the Ghetto needs clearing from time to time by some kind of mysterious explosion, something potent in its workings. Something forces the dreams of the subconscious up into the light of day – like a lightning stroke – giving rise to an object that, could we but read its riddle, symbolises, both in ways and appearance, the mass-soul, could we but understand and interpret the secret language of forms?

'And, just as Nature has her own happenings that foreshadow the advent of the lightning, so do certain forbidding signs portend the arrival of this phantom within our world of fact. The plaster peeling from an old wall will adopt the shape of a running human form; and stony faces stare from the ice-flowers formed by the frost upon the window-panes. Sand from the roof-tops falls in a different way from usual, filling the apprehensive passer-by with the impression it has been thrown by some invisible spirit, trying to form, from the hiding-place where it lurks, all kinds of unfamiliar outlines. No matter what the object one beholds – be it wicker work, all one colour, or the uneven surface of a human skin – we are still obsessed with this disconcerting gift of finding everywhere these ominous, significant shapes, that assume in our dreams the proportion of giants. And always, through these ghostly strivings of these troops of thoughts, endeavouring to gnaw their way through the wall of actuality, runs, like a scarlet thread, a torturing certitude that our own mental consciousness, strive as we may, is being sucked dry, deliberately, that the phantom may attain to concrete form.

'Just now, when I heard Pernath tell how he had met a man clean shaven, with slanting eyes, there stood the Golem before me as I saw it previously.

'He stood there as though risen from the ground. And, for the space of a moment, I was filled with that dumb, familiar fear, the intuition of some ghostly presence near at hand, that I had felt then, in my boyhood, when the Golem had thrown its dread, ominous shadow across my path.

'Sixty-six years ago! And another memory, too, is connected with it – one evening when my sister's fiancé came to settle the marriage date with my family. We amused ourselves by casting lead. I stood by in open-mouthed astonishment, wondering what it all might mean. The childish workings of my mind connected it somehow or other with the Golem, of whom I had often heard my grandfather talk. Every moment I expected to see the door open and the stranger walk into the room.

'My sister filled a ladle with the molten stuff, and emptied it into a bowl of water, laughing the while at my intense excitement. With his withered, trembling hands, my grandfather picked out the lump of lead and held it to the light. Immediately arose a hubbub of excitement. Everybody talked at once; I tried to wriggle through the crowd of agitated guests, but they stopped me.

'Later, when I was older, my father told me how the molten metal had shaped itself into a miniature but quite unmistakable head, smooth and round, as though cast from a mould, with features that bore such an uncanny resemblance to those of the Golem that fear possessed them all.

'Many a time have I discussed the matter with Schemajah Hillel the registrar, who has in his keeping the paraphernalia of the Old Synagogue, together with the clay figure I told you of, from Kaiser Rudolf's days. He has given much time to the Kabbala, and he held the clay image to be nothing but a presage in human form, at the time in which it was made, just as, in my case, was the lump of lead. And the stranger who haunted our precincts he held to be a projection of the thought that had sprung to life in the brain of the old rabbi before he had succeeded in giving it tangible form, and that it could only appear at stated intervals of time, under those astrological conditions in·which it had been created; that then, and then only, would it come back to the earth on its agonised quest for materialisation.

'Hillel's wife, in her lifetime, had also see the Golem face to face, and felt the same shock of paralysis that I had so long as the inexplicable presence was near. She said, too, she was quite positive that what she had seen was her own soul divested of its body; that just for a moment it had stood opposite to her, and gazed into her face with the features of a strange being. In spite of the terrible fear that had got her in its grip, the conviction had never left her that this thing confronting her was only a part of her innermost self.'

'It's not credible,' murmured Prokop, lost in thought.

Vrieslander, too, sat there brooding.

Then came a knock at the door, and the old dame who brings up my evening water, and anything else I happen to want, came in, placed the earthenware pitcher on the floor, and silently withdrew.

We all looked up and gazed vaguely round the room, as though awakening from sleep, though a long time elapsed before any word was spoken.

Some new influence had entered the room with the old crone, and we had first to accustom ourselves to it.

'That red-haired wench, Rosina, too – she has a face that dances for ever before a man's eyes out of the nooks and the crannies.' This from Zwakh, quite suddenly. 'I've known that fixed, grinning smile, now, for a whole generation. First the grandmother ... then the mother! And always the same face ... not a feature altered! The same name, Rosina – one always the resurrection of the other!'

'Isn't Rosina – Aaron Wassertrum's daughter?' I asked.

'So they say,' affirmed Zwakh. 'But Aaron Wassertrum has many a son and many a daughter people know nothing of. Nobody knew who was the father of Rosina's mother, nor what became of her. At the age of fifteen she brought that child into the world, and that was the last heard of her. Her disappearance had something to do with a murder, if I remember rightly, committed in this house on her account.

'Just like her daughter, she turned all the heads of the young men. One of them's alive still – I see him quite often – I can't remember his name. The other all came to a premature end – through her, probably. I only remember detached episodes, here and there, of that bygone time, that stray through my brain like a series of faded pictures. There was one half-witted fellow who used to go from café to café every evening, cutting out silhouettes in black paper for a couple of kreuzer. Once they'd got him drunk he'd sit there in the depths of melancholy sighing and crying, cutting out always the same sharp girl's profile, till his whole stock of paper was all used up. Almost as a child, so they said, he'd been caught in the toils of a certain Rosina – the grandmother, probably, of our one – and loved her so madly he'd lost his reason. When I count the years back, it can't have been anyone but the grandmother of our present Rosina.'

Zwakh ceased speaking and lay back in his chair.

'Fate flits in circles,' thought I, 'around and around this house, returning always to its starting point.' And a hideous image of something I had once seen shot simultaneously into my mind – a cat gone mad, twirling around frantically, in circle after circle.

'Now for the head' – all at once, in Vrieslander's cheery tones. And he took a small billet of wood from his pocket and started to carve.

I pushed my arm-chair into the background, out of the light. My eyes were heavy with weariness.

The hot water for the punch was sizzling in the kettle, and Joshua started to fill our glasses round again. Softly, very softly, the strains of dance-music stole through the closed window; fitfully, now coming, now going, according to the caprices of the wind.

Wouldn't I clink glasses with him? – so the musician wanted to know, after a pause.

But I made no answer. So loth was I to make any kind of movement, I would not even open my mouth. Almost I might have been asleep, such was the feeling of utter quiet that now possessed my soul. I had to glance now and again at the twinkling blade of Vrieslander's pocket-knife, as he cut small chips of the wood, to assure myself I really was awake.

From afar I heard Zwakh's rumbling voice, as he told wonderful stories about puppets, and narrated the plots of his plays.

They were talking now of Dr Savioli, and the elegant lady – some titled man's wife – who paid her clandestine visits to him in that obscure little studio. Once again I saw floating before me the triumphant, mocking visage of Aaron Wassertrum. I wondered if I would confide that experience of mine to Zwakh, then came to the conclusion it would serve no useful purpose, to say nothing of the fact that I knew my will would be unequal to the effort of relating it.

Suddenly I saw all three of them looking at me across the table. 'He is asleep,' said Prokop, so loudly that it sounded almost like a question he had put to me.

Then they spoke in subdued voices, and I realised I was the subject of their conversation.

The blade of Vrieslander's knife danced here and there, catching the light from the lamp, and the glint of it burned into my eyes.

'Mental condition,' were the words I caught. They talked on, and I listened.

'Subjects like the Golem shouldn't be raised in Pernath's company,' said Joshua Prokop reprovingly; 'just now, when he was telling us about the book *Ibbur*, we sat silent and raised no questions. I would wager that it was a dream.'

'Quite right!' Zwakh nodded. 'It's like walking with a lighted candle through a disused room, in which the walls and furniture are all wrapped in dust-sheets, while the dead tinder of the past smothers your footsteps ankle deep; one spark let fall, and fire'll break out of every corner.'

'Was Pernath long in the asylum? Poor devil, anyway ... can't be forty.' Thus Vrieslander.

'I don't know. I haven't the faintest idea where he came from, or what his profession was before. He has all the air of an old-fashioned French aristocrat, with his slender figure and pointed beard. Years ago, an old doctor of my acquaintance asked me to do him a favour, and see if I could procure for a patient of his a lodging somewhere in this street, where no one would be likely to disturb him, or worry him with questions about the past.' Zwakh waved vaguely in my direction. 'Ever since then he's lived here, repairing antiques and cutting precious stones, and apparently making a modest living out of it. It's fortunate for him that he seems to have forgotten everything to do with his mental trouble. You must on no account ask him questions that might awaken his memory. That's what the old doctor used to keep impressing on me. "Remember, Zwakh," he used to say, "all that's over and done with; we've evolved a system now to treat it with; we've built a wall round it, just like fencing in a place where a tragic event has taken place, because of the painful memories." '

The puppeteer's talk struck at me like a pole-axe on a defenceless beast. Red, merciless hands were clutching at my heart. I had had this dumb kind of torment before ... a suspicion that something had been taken away from me, and that I had spent a long time walking at the edge of an abyss, like a sleepwalker. And now the riddle was solved – and burned like an open wound.

That reluctance I had to think of the past ... the strange recurring dream of being in a house with a series of rooms sealed off from me ... the painful inability of my memory to function where associations of my youth were concerned ... all these problems had suddenly achieved their terrible solution: I had been mad, and treated by *hypnosis*. They had, in short, locked up a room which communicated with certain chambers in my brain; they had made me into an exile in the midst of the life that surrounded me.

And no prospect of my ever recovering again that lost portion of my memory.

I understood now that the mainspring of all my thoughts and acts lay hidden in another world, forgotten and never to be recalled; I was like a grafted plant, a twig proceeding from an alien root. Even if I ever did succeed in forcing the door of that locked room, would I not fall immediately a prey to the spirits imprisoned therein?

The story of the Golem as related by Zwakh passed through my mind, and suddenly I recognised a connection of infinite mystery and magnitude between that legendary room without an entrance, which the unknown was supposed to inhabit, and my own significant dream.

That was it! In my case, too, the rope would break, should I but try to glance into that barred window of my inner consciousness.

This curious connection became clearer and clearer within my mind, and the clearer it grew the more terrifying did it become. There were things in the world, so it seemed to me, beyond the mind of man to grasp, riveted indissolubly together and running about distractedly, like blind horses, on a path whose direction is hidden from them.

Here, too, in the Ghetto: a room, the door of which nobody could find; a ghostly presence dwelling therein, that from time to time would walk through the streets, spreading terror and fear in the minds of men!

Vrieslander was still hacking away at his puppethead; you could heard the scraping of his knife upon the wood.

The sound of it somehow distressed me, and I looked up to see if it would not soon be finished.

The head, turning about as it did in the carver's hand, looked alive. It seemed to be peering into all the corners of the room. At last its eyes rested upon me. It appeared pleased to have found me at last.

And I, in my turn, was unable to turn my eyes away. Stonily I stared at that little wooden face.

The carver's knife seemed to hesitate a little, then suddenly made a strong, decided cut, informing the wooden head, all at once, with terrifying personality. I recognised the yellow countenance of the stranger who had brought me the book.

There my powers of discernment ended. It had lasted only one moment, but I could feel my heart cease to beat, and then bound forward agonisingly.

The face, none the less, remained in my mind. Just as it had done before.

It was I myself ... I and none other ... and I lay there on Vrieslander's lap, gaping.

My eyes were wandering round the room, and strange fingers laid their touch upon my head.

All of a sudden I was aware of Zwakh's face distorted with excitement. I could hear his voice: 'God! It's the Golem!'

A short struggle had ensued, while they had tried to wrest Vrieslander's work from his hand. But he fended them off, and crying, with a laugh: 'All right! I've made a mess of this job,' had opened the window and flung the head into the street below.

Consciousness left me, and I drove into deep darkness veined with shimmering golden threads, and when I awoke again, as it seemed, after a long, long time, I heard the wooden head strike the pavement outside.

'Wake up,' I could hear Joshua Prokop saying to me. 'You've been so fast asleep you couldn't feel how we've been shaking you. We've finished the punch, and you've missed all the fun.'

Then the sharp pain of what I had just been hearing surged over me once more, and I wanted to shriek aloud that it was not a dream that I had told them of the book *Ibbur* – that I would take it out of its box and show it to them.

But I could neither utter these thoughts nor combat the genral spirit of leave-taking that had now seized my guests.

Zwakh forcefully put my cloak round my shoulders while he cried: 'Come along with us now to Loisitschek's, Master Pernath. It'll cheer you up!'

XIII

The Old Nurse's Story

Elizabeth Gaskell

BBC Radio has also continued to give its listeners a regular diet of supernatural plays and stories – with the Book At Bedtime *and* Spinechillers *series of recent years being particularly noteworthy and making good use of the classic tales of fear. However, while the American programme* Mystery Theatre *has made a point of updating and changing many of its stories,* Spinechillers *in particular has remained faithful to the original texts. The programme's scriptwriters have certainly cut away some of the verbiage from the old stories, but the period atmosphere and manners have been faithfully preserved – with splendid and chilling effect. Indeed, the shade of that old pioneer, A.J.Alan, must be very delighted at the way the high standards he set half a century ago are being maintained! A recent outstanding production was 'The Old Nurse's Story' by the Victorian writer Mrs Gaskell, famous for her novels* Cranford *(1853) and* North and South *(1854). Elizabeth Cleghorn Gaskell (1810-1865) was also highly-regarded as a ghost story writer during her lifetime and contributed a number of these to Charles Dickens' special Christmas editions of his magazines. 'The Old Nurse's Story' was actually the first of these stories and was notable when first published in* Household Words *at Christmas 1852 for the twist ending which lifted it above the conventional thrillers of the day. With the passing of time, it has come to be seen as the epitome of the Victorian ghost story, and according to E.F.Bleiler, an expert on supernatural fiction, is 'perhaps an ultimate source, indirectly, for* The Turn of the Screw'. *The* Spinechiller *version was produced in two memorable parts by Kay Patrick, with Valerie Windsor narrating the garrulous old nurse's tale of strange sights and sounds in a house with a terrible secret. Although the story may be well over a hundred years old, it has a fascination which will surely make it intriguing and entertaining for many more years to come. And as long as there is material of this quality to be broadcast in radio's own unique way, I am sure there will equally always be a place for the wireless receiver in our homes. There certainly will be in mine!*

You know, my dears, that your mother was an orphan, and an only child; and I dare say you have heard that your grandfather was a clergyman up in Westmorland, where I come from. I was just a girl in the village school, when, one day, your grandmother came in to ask the mistress if there was any scholar there who would do for a nurse-maid; and mighty proud I was, I can tell ye, when the mistress called me up, and spoke to my being a good girl at my needle, and a steady, honest girl, and one whose parents were very respectable, though they might be poor. I thought I should like nothing better than to serve the pretty young lady, who was blushing as deep as I was as she spoke of the coming baby, and what I should have to do with it. However, I see you don't care so much for this part of my story as for what you think is to come, so I'll tell you at once. I was engaged and settled at the parsonage before Miss Rosamond (that was the baby, who is now your mother) was born. To be sure, I had little enough to do with her when she came, for she was never out of her mother's arms, and slept by her all night long; and proud enough was I sometimes when missis trusted her to me.

There never was such a baby before or since, though you've all of you been fine enough in your turns; but for sweet, winning ways, you've none of you come up to your mother. She took after her mother, who was a real lady born; a Miss Furnivall, a grand-daughter of Lord Furnivall's, in Northumberland. I believe she had neither brother nor sister, and had been brought up in my lord's family till she had married your grandfather, who was just a curate, son to a shopkeeper in Carlisle – but a clever, fine gentleman as ever was – and one who was a right-down hard worker in his parish, which was very wide, and scattered all abroad over the Westmorland Fells. When your mother, little Miss Rosamond, was about four or five years old, both her parents died in a fortnight – one after the other. Ah! that was a sad time. My pretty young mistress and me was looking for another baby, when my master came home from one of his long rides, wet and tired, and took the fever he died of; and then she never held up her head again, but just lived to see her dead baby, and have it laid on her breast before she sighed away her life. My mistress had asked me, on her death-bed, never to leave Miss Rosamond; but if she had never spoken a word, I would have gone with the little child to the end of the world.

The next thing, and before we had well stilled our sobs, the executors and guardians came to settle the affairs. They were my poor young mistress's own cousin, Lord Furnivall, and Mr Esthwaite, my master's brother, a shopkeeper in Manchester; not so well-to-do then as he was afterwards, and with a large family rising about him. Well! I don't know if it were their settling, or because of a letter my mistress wrote on her death-bed to her cousin, my lord; but somehow it was settled that Miss Rosamond and me were to go to Furnivall Manor House, in Northumberland, and my lord spoke as if it had been her mother's wish that she should live with his family, and as if he had no objections, for that one or two more or less could make no difference in so grand a household. So though that was not the way in which I should have wished the coming of my bright and pretty pet to have been looked at – who was like a sunbeam to any family, be it never so grand – I was well pleased that all the folks in the Dale should stand and admire when they heard I was going to be young lady's maid at my Lord Furnivall's at Furnivall Manor.

But I made a mistake in thinking we were to go and live where my lord did. It turned out that the family had left Furnivall Manor House fifty years or more. I could not hear that my poor young mistress had ever been there, though she had been brought up in the family; and I was sorry for that, for I should have liked Miss Rosamond's youth to have passed where her mother's had been.

My lord's gentleman, from whom I asked so many questions as I durst, said that the Manor House was at the foot of the Cumberland Fells, and a very grand place; that an old Miss Furnivall, a great-aunt of my lord's, lived there, with only a few servants; but that it was a very healthy place, and my lord had thought that it would suit Miss Rosamond very well for a few years, and that her being there might perhaps amuse his old aunt.

I was bidden by my lord to have Miss Rosamond's things ready by a certain day. He was a stern, proud man, as they say all the Lords Furnivall were; and he never spoke a word more than was necessary. Folk did say he had loved my young mistress; but that, because she knew that his father would object, she would never listen to him, and married Mr Esthwaite; but I don't know. He never married, at any rate. But he never took much notice of Miss Rosamond; which I thought he might have done if he had cared for her dead mother. He sent his gentleman with us to Manor House, telling him to join him at Newcastle that same evening; so there was no great length of time for him to make us known to all the strangers before he, too, shook us off; and we were left, two lonely young things (I was not eighteen), in the great, old Manor House.

It seems like yesterday that we drove there. We had left our own dear parsonage very early, and we had both cried as if our hearts would break, though we were travelling in my lord's carriage, which I thought so much of once. And now it was long past noon on a September day, and we stopped to change horses for the last time at a little smoky town all full of colliers and miners. Miss Rosamond had fallen asleep, but Mr Henry told me to waken her, that she might see the park and the Manor House as we drove up. I thought it rather a pity; but I did what he bade me, for fear he should complain of me to my lord. We had left all signs of a town, or even a village, and were then inside the gates of a large wild park – not like the parks here in the north, but with rocks, and the noise of running water, and gnarled thorn-trees, and old oaks, all white and peeled with age.

The road went up about two miles, and then we saw a great and stately house, with many trees close around it, so close that in some places their branches dragged against the walls when the wind blew; and some hung broken down; for no one seemed to take much charge of the place; to lop the wood, or to keep the moss-covered carriage-way in order. Only in front of the house all was clear. The great oval drive was without a weed; and neither tree nor creeper was allowed to grow over the long, many-windowed front; at both sides of which a wing projected, which were each the ends of other side fronts; for the house, although it was so desolate, was even grander than I expected. Behind it rose the Fells, which seemed unenclosed and bare enough; and on the left-hand of the house, as you stood facing it, was a little, old-fashioned flower-garden, as I found out afterwards. A door opened out upon it from the west front; it had been scooped out of the thick dark wood for some old Lady Furnivall; but the branches of the great forest trees had grown and overshadowed it again, and there were very few flowers that would live there at that time.

When we drove up the great front entrance, and went into the hall I thought we should be lost – it was so large, and vast, and grand. There was a chandelier, all of bronze, hung down from the middle of the ceiling; and I had never seen one before, and looked at it all in amaze. Then, at one end of the hall, was a great fire-place, as large as the sides of the houses in my country, with massy andirons and dogs to hold the wood; and by it were heavy, old-fashioned sofas. At the opposite end of the hall, to the left as you went in – on the western side – was an organ built into the wall, and so large that it filled up the best part of that end. Beyond it, on the same side, was a door; and opposite, on each side of the fireplace, were also doors leading to the east front; but those I never went through as long as I stayed in the house, so I can't tell you what lay beyond.

The afternoon was closing in, and the hall, which had no fire lighted in it, looked dark and gloomy, but we did not stay there a moment. The old servant, who had opened the door for us, bowed to Mr Henry, and took us in through the door at the farther side if the great organ, and led us through several smaller halls and passages into the west drawing-room, where he said that Miss Furnivall was sitting. Poor little Miss Rosamond held very tight to me, as if she were scared and lost in that great place, and as for myself, I was not much better. The west drawing-room was very cheerful-looking, with a warm fire in it, and plenty of wood, comfortable furniture about. Miss Furnivall was an old lady not far from eighty, I should think, but I do not know. She was thin and tall, and had a face as full of fine wrinkles as if they had been drawn all over it with a needle's point. Her eyes were very watchful, to make up, I suppose, for her being so deaf as to be obliged to use a trumpet.

Sitting with her, working at the same great piece of tapestry, was Mrs Stark, her maid and companion, and almost as old as she was. She had lived with Miss Furnivall ever since they were both young, and now she seemed more like a friend than a servant; she looked so cold and grey and stony – as if she had never loved or cared for anyone; and I don't suppose she did care for anyone except her mistress; and, owing to the great deafness of the latter, Mrs Stark treated her very much as if she were a child. Mr Henry gave some message from my lord, and then he bowed good-bye to us all – taking no notice of my sweet little Miss Rosamond's outstretched hand – and left us standing there, being looked at by the two old ladies through their spectacles.

I was right glad when they rung for the old footman who had shown us in at first, and told him to take us to our rooms. So we went out of that great drawing-room, and into another sitting-room, and out of that, and then up a great flight of stairs, and along a broad gallery – which was something like a library, having books all down one side and windows and writing-tables all down the other – till we came to our rooms, which I was not sorry to hear were just over the kitchens; for I began to think I should be lost in that wilderness of a house. There was an old nursery that had been used for all the little lords and ladies long ago, with a pleasant fire burning in the grate, and the kettle boiling on the hob, and tea-things spread out on the table; and out of that room was the night-nursery, with a little crib for Miss Rosamond close to my bed. And old James called up Dorothy, his wife, to bid us welcome; and both he and she were so hospitable and kind that by and by Miss Rosamond and me felt quite at home; and by the time tea was over, she was sitting on Dorothy's knee, and chattering away as fast as her little tongue could go.

I soon found out that Dorothy was from Westmorland, and that bound her and me together, as it were; and I would never wish to meet with kinder people than were old James and his wife. James had lived pretty nearly all his life in my lord's family, and thought there was no one so grand as they. He even looked down a little on his wife; because, till he had married her, she had never lived in any but a farmer's household. But he was very fond of her, as well he might be. They had one servant under them, to do all the rough work. Agnes, they called her; and she and me and James and Dorothy, with Miss Furnivall and Mrs Stark, made up the family; always remembering my sweet little Miss Rosamond. I used to wonder what they had done before she came, they thought so much of her now. Kitchen and drawing-room, it was all the same. The hard, sad Miss Furnivall, and the cold Mrs Stark, looked pleased when she came fluttering in like a bird, playing and pranking hither and thither, with a continual murmur, and pretty prattle of gladness. I am sure, they were sorry many a time when she flitted away into the kitchen, though they were too proud to ask her to stay with them, and were a little surprised at her taste; though to be sure, as Mrs Stark said, it was not to be wondered at, remembering what stock her father had come of.

The great, old rambling house was a famous place for little Miss Rosamond. She made expeditions all over it, with me at her heels; all except the east wing, which was never opened, and whither we never thought of going. But in the western and northern part was many a pleasant room; full of things that were curiosities to us, though they might not have been to people who had seen more. The windows were darkened by the sweeping boughs of the trees, and the ivy which had overgrown them: but, in the green gloom, we could manage to see old China jars and carved ivory boxes, and great heavy books, and, above all, the old pictures.

Once, I remember, my darling would have Dorothy go with us to tell us who they all were; for they were all portraits of some of my lord's family, though Dorothy could not tell us the names of every one. We had gone through most of the rooms, when we came to the old state drawing-room over the hall, and there was a picture of Miss Furnivall; or, as she was called in those days, Miss Grace, for she was the younger sister. Such a beauty she must have been! but with such a set, proud look, and such scorn looking out of her handsome eyes, with her eyebrows just a little raised, as if she were wondering how anyone could have the impertinence to look at her; and her lip curled at us, as we stood there gazing. She had a dress on, the like of which I had never seen before, but it was all the fashion when she was young: a hat of some soft white stuff like beaver, pulled a little over her brows, and a beautiful plume of feathers sweeping round it on one side; and her gown of blue satin was open in front to a quilted white stomacher.

'Well, to be sure!' said I, when I had gazed my fill. 'Flesh is grass, they do say; but who would have thought that Miss Furnivall had been such an out-and-out beauty, to see her now?'

'Yes,' said Dorothy. 'Folks change sadly. But if what my master's father used to say was true, Miss Furnivall, the elder sister, was handsomer than Miss Grace. Her picture is here somewhere; but, if I show it to you, you must never let on, even to James, that you have seen it. Can the little lady hold her tongue, think you?' asked she.

I was not so sure, for she was such a little sweet, bold, open-spoken child, so I set her to hide herself; and then I helped Dorothy to turn a great picture, that leaned with its face towards the wall, and was not hung up as the others were. To be sure, it beat Miss Grace for beauty; and, I think, for scornful pride too, though in that matter it might be hard to choose. I could have looked at it an hour, but Dorothy seemed half frightened at having shown it to me, and hurried it back again, and bade me run and find Miss Rosamond, for that there were some ugly places about the house, where she should like ill for the child to go. I was a brave, high-spirited girl, and thought little of what the old woman said, for I liked hide-and-seek as well as any child in the parish; so off I ran to find my little one.

As winter drew on, and the days grew shorter, I was sometimes almost certain that I heard a noise as if someone was playing on the great organ in the hall. I did not hear it every evening; but, certainly, I did very often; usually when I was sitting with Miss Rosamond, after I had put her to bed, and keeping quite still and silent in the bedroom. Then I used to hear it booming and swelling away in the distance. The first night, when I went down to my supper, I asked Dorothy who had been playing music, and James said shortly that I was a gowk to take the wind soughing among the trees for music; but

I saw Dorothy look at him very fearfully, and Bessy, the kitchen-maid, said something beneath her breath, and went quite white. I saw they did not like my question, so I held my peace till I was with Dorothy alone, when I knew I could get a good deal out of her.

So, the next day, I watched my time, and I coaxed and asked her who it was that played the organ; for I knew that it was the organ and not the wind well enough, for all I had kept silence before James. But Dorothy had had her lesson, I'll warrant, and never a word could I get from her. So then I tried Bessy, though I had always held my head rather above her, as I was evened to James and Dorothy, for she was little better than their servant. So she said I must never, never tell; and if I ever told, I was never to say *she* had told me; but it was a very strange noise, and she had heard it many a time, but most of all on winter nights, and before storms; and folks did say, it was the old lord playing on the great organ in the hall, just as he used to do when he was alive; but who the old lord was, or why he played, and why he played on stormy winter evenings in particular, she either could not or would not tell me. Well! I told you I had a brave heart; and I thought it was rather pleasant to have that grand music rolling about the house, let who would be the player; for now it rose above the great gusts of wind, and wailed and triumphed just like a living creature, and then it fell to a softness most complete; only it was always music and tunes, so it was nonsense to call it the wind.

I thought at first that it might be Miss Furnivall who played, unknown to Bessy; but one day when I was in the hall by myself, I opened the organ and peeped all about it and around it, as I had done to the organ in Crosthwaite Church once before, and I saw it was all broken and destroyed inside, though it looked so brave and fine; and then, though it was noonday, my flesh began to creep a little, and I shut it up, and ran away pretty quickly to my own bright nursery; and I did not like hearing the music for some time after that, any more than James and Dorothy did.

All this time Miss Rosamond was making herself more and more beloved. The old ladies liked her to dine with them at their early dinner; James stood behind Miss Furnivall's chair, and I behind Miss Rosamond's all in state; and, after dinner, she would play about in a corner of the great drawing-room, as still as any mouse, while Miss Furnivall slept, and I had my dinner in the kitchen. But she was glad enough to come to me in the nursery afterwards; for, as she said, Miss Furnivall was so sad, and Mrs Stark so dull; but she and I were merry enough; and, by and by, I got not to care for that weird, rolling music, which did one no harm, if we did not know where it came from.

That winter was very cold. In the middle of October the frosts began, and lasted many, many weeks. I remember, one day at dinner, Miss Furnivall lifted up her sad, heavy eyes and said to Mrs Stark, 'I am afraid we shall have a terrible winter,' in a strange kind of meaning way. But Mrs Stark pretended not to hear, and talked very loud of something else. My little lady and I did not care for the frost; not we! As long as it was dry we climbed up the steep brows, behind the house, and went up on the Fells, which were bleak, and bare enough, and where we ran races in the fresh, sharp air; and once we came down by a new path that took us past the two old gnarled holly trees, which grew about half way down by the east side of the house.

But the days grew shorter and shorter; and the old lord – if it was he – played more and more stormily and sadly on the great organ. One Sunday afternoon – it must have been towards the end of November – I asked Dorothy to take charge of little Missy when she came out of the drawing-room, after Miss Furnivall had had her nap; for it was too cold to take her with me to church, and yet I wanted to go. And Dorothy was glad enough to promise, and was so fond of the child that all seemed well; and Bessy and I set off briskly, though the sky hung heavy and black over the white earth, as if the night had never fully gone away; and the air, though still, was very biting and keen.

'We shall have a fall of snow,' said Bessy to me. And sure enough, even while we were in church, it came down thick, in great, large flakes, so thick it almost darkened the windows. It had stopped snowing before we came out, but it lay soft, thick, and deep beneath our feet as we tramped home. Before we got to the hall the moon rose, and I think it was lighter then – what with the moon, and what with the white dazzling snow – than it had been when we went to church, between two and three o'clock. I have not told you that Miss Furnivall and Mrs Stark never went to church; they used to read the prayers together, in their quiet, gloomy way; they seemed to feel the Sunday very long with their tapestry-work to be busy at.

So when I went to Dorothy in the kitchen, to fetch Miss Rosamond and take her upstairs with me, I did not much wonder when the old woman told me that the ladies had kept the child with them, and that she had never come to the kitchen, as I had bidden her when she was tired of behaving pretty in the drawing-room. So I took off my things and went to find her, and bring her to her supper in the nursery. But when I went into the best drawing-room there sat the two old ladies, very still and quiet, dropping out a word now and then but looking as if nothing so bright and merry as Miss Rosamond had ever been near them. Still I thought she might be hiding from me; it was one of her pretty ways; and that she had persuaded them to look as if they knew nothing about her; so I went softly peeping under this sofa, and behind that chair, making believe I was sadly frightened at not finding her.

'What's the matter, Hester?' said Mrs Stark sharply. I don't know if Miss Furnivall had seen me, for, as I told you, she was very deaf, and she sat quite still, idly staring into the fire, with her hopeless face. 'I'm only looking for my little Rosy-Posy,' I replied, still thinking that the child was there, and near me, though I could not see her.

'Miss Rosamond is not here,' said Mrs Stark. 'She went away more than an hour ago to find Dorothy.' And she too turned and went on looking into the fire.

My heart sank at this, and I began to wish I had never left my darling. I went back to Dorothy and told her. James was gone out for the day, but she and me and Bessy took lights and went up into the nursery first, and then we roamed over the great large house, calling and entreating Miss Rosamond to come out of her hiding-place, and not frighten us to death in that way. But there was no answer; no sound.

'Oh!' said I at last. 'Can she have got into the east wing and hidden there?'

But Dorothy said it was not possible, for that she herself had never been there; that the doors were always locked, and my lord's steward had the keys, she believed; at any rate, neither

she nor James had ever seen them. So I said I would go back
and see if, after all, she was not hidden in the drawing-room,
unknown to the old ladies; and if I found her there I said I
would whip her well for the fright she had given me; but I
never meant to do it. Well, I went back to the west
drawing-room, and I told Mrs Stark we could not find her
anywhere, and asked for leave to look all about the furniture
there, for I thought now, that she might have fallen asleep in
some warm hidden corner; but no! we looked, Miss Furnivall
got up and looked, trembling all over, and she was nowhere
there; then we set off again, everyone in the house, and looked
in all the places we had searched before, but we could not find
her. Miss Furnivall shivered and shook so much that Mrs Stark
took her back into the warm drawing-room; but not before
they made me promise to bring her to them when she was
found. Welladay! I began to think she never would be found,
when I bethought me to look out into the great front court, all
covered with snow.

I was upstairs when I looked out; but it was such clear
moonlight I could see, quite plain, two little footprints, which
might be traced from the hall door and round the corner of the
east wing. I don't know how I got down, but I tugged open the
great, stiff hall door; and, throwing the skirt of my gown over
my head for a cloak, I ran out. I turned the east corner, and
there a black shadow fell on the snow; but when I came again
into the moonlight, there were the little foot-marks going up –
up to the Fells. It was bitter cold; so cold that the air almost
took the skin off my face as I ran, but I ran on, crying to think
how my poor little darling must be perished and frightened. I
was within sight of the holly trees when I saw a shepherd
coming down the hill, bearing something in his arms wrapped
in his maud. He shouted to me, and asked me if I had lost a
bairn; and, when I could not speak for crying, he bore towards
me, and I saw my wee bairnie lying still, and white, and stiff, in
his arms, as if she had been dead. He told me he had been up
the Fells to gather in his sheep, before the deep cold of night
came on, and that under the holly trees (black marks on the
hill-side, where no other bush was for miles around) he had
found my little lady – my lamb – my queen – my darling – stiff
and cold, in the terrible sleep which is frost-begotten.

Oh, the joy, and the tears of having her in my arms once again! for I would not let him carry her; but took her, maud and all, into my own arms, and held her near my own warm neck and heart, and felt the life stealing slowly back again into her little gentle limbs. But she was still insensible when we reached the hall, and I had no breath for speech. We went in by the kitchen door.

'Bring the warming-pan,' said I; and I carried her upstairs, and began undressing her by the nursery fire, which Bessy had kept up. I called my little lammie all the sweet and playful names I could think of – even while my eyes were blinded by my tears; and at last, oh! at length she opened her large, blue eyes. Then I put her into her warm bed, and sent Dorothy down to tell Miss Furnivall that all was well; and I made up my mind to sit by my darling's bedside the live-long night. She fell away into a soft sleep as soon as her pretty head had touched the pillow, and I watched by her until morning light; when she wakened up bright and clear – or so I thought at first – and, my dears, so I think now.

She said that she had fancied that she should like to go to Dorothy, for that both the old ladies were asleep, and it was very dull in the drawing-room; and that, as she was going through the west lobby, she saw the snow through the high window falling – falling – soft and steady. But she wanted to see it lying pretty and white on the ground; so she made her way into the great hall; and then, going to the window, she saw it bright and soft upon the drive; but while she stood there, she saw a little girl, not so old as she was, 'but so pretty,' said my darling, 'and this little girl beckoned to me to come out; and oh, she was so pretty and so sweet, I could not choose but go.' And then this other little girl had taken her by the hand, and side by side the two had gone round the east corner.

'Now you are a naughty little girl, and telling stories,' said I. 'What would your good mamma, that is in heaven, and never told a story in her life, say to her little Rosamond, if she heard her – and I dare say she does – telling stories!'

'Indeed, Hester,' sobbed out my child, 'I'm telling you true. Indeed I am.'

'Don't tell me!' said I, very stern. 'I tracked you by your foot-marks through the snow; there were only yours to be seen; and if you had had a little girl to go hand in hand with you up the hill, don't you think the footprints would have gone along with yours?'

'I can't help it, dear, dear Hester,' said she, crying, 'if they did not. I never looked at her feet, but she held my hand fast and tight in her little one, and it was very, very cold. She took me up the Fell path, up to the holly trees; and there I saw a lady weeping and crying; but when she saw me, she hushed her weeping, and smiled very proud and grand, and took me on her knee, and began to lull me to sleep; and that's all, Hester – but that is true; and my dear mamma knows it is,' said she, crying. So I thought the child was in a fever, and pretended to believe her, as she went over her story – over and over again, and always the same. At last Dorothy knocked at the door with Miss Rosamond's breakfast; and she told me the old ladies were down in the eating-parlour, and that they wanted to speak to me. They had both been into the night-nursery the evening before, but it was after Miss Rosamond was asleep; so they had only looked at her – not asked me any questions.

'I shall catch it,' thought I to myself, as I went along the north gallery. 'And yet,' I thought, taking courage, 'it was in their charge I left her; and it's they that's to blame for letting her steal away unknown and unwatched.' So I went in boldly, and told my story. I told it all to Miss Furnivall, shouting it close to her ear; but when I came to the mention of the other little girl out in the snow, coaxing and tempting her out, and willing her up to the grand and beautiful lady by the holly tree, she threw her arms up – her old and withered arms – and cried aloud, 'Oh! Heaven, forgive! Have mercy!'

Mrs Stark took hold of her; roughly enough, I thought; but she was past Mrs Stark's management, and spoke to me, in a kind of wild warning and authority.

'Hester, keep her from that child! It will lure her to her death! That evil child! Tell her it is a wicked, naughty child.' Then Mrs Stark hurried me out of the room; where, indeed, I was glad enough to go; but Miss Furnivall kept shrieking out, 'Oh! have mercy! Wilt Thou never forgive! It is many a long year ago –'

I was very uneasy in my mind after that. I durst never leave Miss Rosamond, night or day, for fear lest she might slip off again, after some fancy or other; and all the more because I thought I could make out that Miss Furnivall was crazy, from their odd ways about her; and I was afraid lest something of the same kind (which might be in the family, you know) hung over my darling. And the great frost never ceased all the time; and whenever it was a more stormy night than usual, between the gusts, and through the wind, we heard the old lord playing on the great organ. But, old lord or not, wherever Miss Rosamond went, there I followed; for my love for her, pretty, helpless orphan, was stronger than my fear for the grand and terrible sound. Besides, it rested with me to keep her cheerful and merry, as beseemed her age. So we played together, and wandered together, here and there, and everywhere; for I never dared to lose sight of her again in that large and rambling house. And so it happened, that one afternoon, not long before Christmas Day, we were playing together on the billiard-table in the great hall (not that we knew the way of playing, but she liked to roll the smooth, ivory balls with her pretty hands, and I liked to do whatever she did); and, by and by, without our noticing it, it grew dusk indoors, though it was still light in the open air, and I was thinking of taking her back into the nursery, when, all of a sudden, she cried out:

'Look! Hester, look! there is my poor little girl out in the snow!'

I turned towards the long narrow windows, and there, sure enough, I saw a little girl, less than my Miss Rosamond – dressed all unfit to be out of doors such a bitter night – crying, and beating against the window-panes, as if she wanted to be let in. She seemed to sob and wail, till Miss Rosamond could bear it no longer, and was flying to the door to open it, when, all of a sudden, and close up upon us, the great organ pealed out so loud and thundering, it fairly made me tremble; and all the more, when I remembered me that, even in the stillness of that dead-cold weather, I had heard no sound of little battering hands upon the window glass, although the Phantom Child had seemed to put forth all its force; and, although I had seen it wail and cry, no faintest touch of sound had fallen upon my ears. Whether I remembered all this at the very moment, I do not know; the great organ sound had so stunned me into terror; but this I know: I caught up Miss Rosamond before she got the hall door opened, and clutched her, and carried her away, kicking and screaming, into the large bright kitchen, where Dorothy and Agnes were busy with their mince pies.

'What is the matter with my sweet one?' cried Dorothy, as I bore in Miss Rosamond, who was sobbing as if her heart would break.

'She won't let me open the door for my little girl to come in; and she'll die if she is out on the Fells all night. Cruel, naughty Hester,' she said, slapping me; but she might have struck harder, for I had seen a look of ghastly terror on Dorothy's face, which made my very blood run cold.

'Shut the back-kitchen door fast, and bolt it well,' said she to Agnes. She said no more; she gave me raisins and almonds to quiet Miss Rosamond; but she sobbed about the little girl in the snow, and would not touch any of the good things. I was thankful when she cried herself to sleep in bed. Then I stole down to the kitchen, and told Dorothy I had made up my mind. I would carry my darling back to my father's house in Applethwaite; where, if we lived humbly, we lived at peace. I said I had been frightened enough with the old lord's organ-playing; but now that I had seen for myself this little moaning child, all decked out as no child in the neighbourhood could be, beating and battering to get in, yet always without any sound or noise – with the dark wound on her right shoulder; and that Miss Rosamond had known it again for the phantom that had nearly lured her to her death (which Dorothy knew was true); I would stand it no longer.

I saw Dorothy change colour once or twice. When I had done she told me she did not think I could take Miss Rosamond with me, for that she was my lord's ward, and I had no right over her; and she asked me, would I leave the child that I was so fond of just for sounds and sights that could do me no harm; and that they had all had to get used to in their turns? I was all in a hot, trembling passion; and I said it was very well for her to talk, that knew what these sights and noises betokened, and that had, perhaps, had something to do with the Spectre-Child while it was alive. And I taunted her so, that she told me all she knew, at last; and then I wished I had never been told, for it only made me afraid more than ever.

She said she had heard the tale from old neighbours, that

were alive when she was first married; when folks used to come
to the hall sometimes, before it had got such a bad name on
the country-side: it might not be true, or it might, what she
had been told.

The old lord was Miss Furnivall's father – Miss Grace as
Dorothy called her, for Miss Maude was the elder, and Miss
Furnivall by rights. The old lord was eaten up with pride. Such
a proud man was never seen or heard of; and his daughters
were like him. No one was good enough to wed them,
although they had choice enough; for they were the great
beauties of their day, as I had seen by their portraits where they
hung in the state drawing-room. But, as the old saying is,
'Pride will have a fall'; and these two haughty beauties fell in
love with the same man, and he no better than a foreign
musician whom their father had down from London to play
music with him at the Manor House. For above all things, next
to his pride, the old lord loved music. He could play on nearly
every instrument that ever was heard of: and it was a strange
thing it did not soften him; but he was a fierce, dour old man,
and had broken his poor wife's heart with his cruelty, they said.
He was mad after music, and would pay any money for it. So
he got this foreigner to come; who made such beautiful music,
that they said the very birds on the trees stopped their singing
to listen. And, by degrees, this foreign gentleman got such a
hold over the old lord that nothing would serve him but that
he must come every year; and it was he that had the great
organ brought from Holland and built up in the hall, where it
stood now. He taught the old lord to play on it; but many and
many a time, when Lord Furnivall was thinking of nothing but
his fine organ, and his finer music, the dark foreigner was
walking abroad in the woods with one of the young ladies;
now Miss Maude, and then Miss Grace.

Miss Maude won the day and carried off the prize – such as it
was; and he and she were married, all unknown to anyone;
and before he made his next yearly visit, she had been confined
of a little girl at a farm-house on the Moors, while her father
and Miss Grace thought she was away at Doncaster Races. But
though she was a wife and a mother she was not a bit softened,
but as haughty and as passionate as ever; and perhaps more so,
for she was jealous of Miss Grace, to whom her foreign

husband paid a deal of court – by way of blinding her – as he told his wife. But Miss Grace triumphed over Miss Maude, and Miss Maude grew fiercer and fiercer, both with her husband and with her sister; and the former – who could easily shake off what was disagreeable, and hide himself in foreign countries – went away a month before his usual time that summer, and half threatened that he would never come back again.

Meanwhile, the little girl was left at the farm-house, and her mother used to have her horse saddled and gallop wildly over the hills to see her once every week at the very least – for where she loved, she loved; and where she hated, she hated. And the old lord went on playing – playing on his organ; and the servants thought the sweet music he made had soothed down his awful temper, of which (Dorothy said) some terrible tales could be told. He grew infirm too, and had to walk with a crutch; and his son – that was the present Lord Furnivall's father – was with the army in America, and the other son at sea; so Miss Maude had it pretty much her own way, and she and Miss Grace grew colder and bitterer to each other every day; till at last they hardly ever spoke, except when the old lord was by. The foreign musician came again the next summer, but it was for the last time; for they led him such a life with their jealousy and their passions that he grew weary, and went away, and never was heard of again. And Miss Maude, who had always meant to have her marriage acknowledged when her father should be dead, was left now a deserted wife – whom nobody knew to have been married – with a child that she dared not own, although she loved it to distraction; living with a father whom she feared, and a sister whom she hated.

When the next summer passed over and the dark foreigner never came, both Miss Maude and Miss Grace grew gloomy and sad; they had a haggard look about them, though they looked handsome as ever. But by and by Miss Maude brightened; for her father grew more and more infirm, and more than ever carried away by his music; and she and Miss Grace lived almost entirely apart, having separate rooms, the one on the west side, Miss Maude on the east – those very rooms which were now shut up. So she thought she might have her little girl with her, and no one need ever know except those who dared not speak about it, and were bound to believe that it was, as she said, a cottager's child she had taken a fancy to. All this, Dorothy said, was pretty well known; but what came afterwards no one knew, except Miss Grace and Mrs Stark, who was even then her maid, and much more of a friend to her than ever her sister had been. But the servants supposed, from words that were dropped, that Miss Maude had triumphed over Miss Grace, and told her that all the time the dark foreigner had been mocking her with pretended love he was her own husband; the colour left Miss Grace's cheek and lips that very day for ever, and she was heard to say many a time that sooner or later she would have her revenge; and Mrs Stark was for ever spying about the east rooms.

One fearful night, just after the New Year had come in, when the snow was lying thick and deep, and the flakes were still falling – fast enough to blind any one who might be out and abroad – there was a great and violent noise heard, and the old lord's voice above all, cursing and swearing awfully; and the cries of a little child; and the proud defiance of a fierce woman; and the sound of a blow; and a dead stillness; and moans and wailings dying away on the hill-side! Then the old lord summoned all his servants, and told them, with terrible oaths, and words more terrible, that his daughter had disgraced herself, and that he had turned her out of doors – her, and her child – and that if ever they gave her help, or food, or shelter, he prayed that they might never enter heaven. And, all the while, Miss Grace stood by him, white and still as any stone; and when he had ended she heaved a great sigh, as much as to say her work was done, and her end was accomplished. But the old lord never touched his organ again, and died within the year; and no wonder! for, on the morrow of that wild and fearful night, the shepherds, coming down the Fell side, found Miss Maude sitting, all crazy and smiling, under the holly trees, nursing a dead child – with a terrible mark on its right shoulder. 'But that was not what killed it,' said Dorothy; 'it was the frost and the cold. Every wild creature was in its hole, and every beast in its fold – while the child and its mother were turned out to wander on the Fells! And now you know all, and I wonder if you are less frightened now?'

I was more frightened than ever; but I said I was not. I wished Miss Rosamond and myself well out of that dreadful house for ever; but I would not leave her, and I dared not take her away. But oh! how I watched her, and guarded her! We bolted the doors and shut the window-shutters fast, and an hour or more before dark rather than leave them open five minutes too late. But my little lady still heard the weird child crying and mourning; and not all we could do or say could keep her from wanting to go to her, and let her in from the cruel wind and the snow. All this time, I kept away from Miss Furnivall and Mrs Stark as much as ever I could; for I feared them – I knew no good could be about them, with their grey, hard faces, and their dreamy eyes looking back into the ghastly years that were gone. But, even in my fear, I had a kind of pity – for Miss Furnivall, at least. Those gone down to the pit can hardly have a more hopeless look than that which was ever on her face. At last I even got so sorry for her – who never said a word but what was quite forced from her – that I prayed for her; and I taught Miss Rosamond to pray for one who had done a deadly sin; but often, when she came to those words, she would listen, and start up from her knees, and say, 'I hear my little girl plaining and crying very sad – Oh! let her in, or she will die!'

One night – just after New Year's Day had come at last, and the long winter had taken a turn, as I hoped – I heard the west drawing-room bell ring three times, which was a signal for me. I would not leave Miss Rosamond alone, for all she was asleep – for the old lord had been playing wilder than ever – and I feared lest my darling should waken to hear the Spectre-Child; see her I knew she could not – I had fastened the windows too well for that. So I took her out of her bed and wrapped her up in such outer clothes as were most handy, and carried her down to the drawing-room, where the old ladies sat at their tapestry-work as usual. They looked up when I came in, and Mrs Stark asked, quite astounded, 'Why did I bring Miss Rosamond there, out of her warm bed?' I had begun to whisper, 'Because I was afraid of her being tempted out while I was away, by the wild child in the snow,' when she stopped me short (with a glance at Miss Furnivall), and said Miss Furnivall wanted me to undo some work she had done wrong, and which neither of them could see to unpick. So I laid my pretty dear on the sofa, and sat down on a stool by them, and hardened my heart against them, as I heard the wind rising and howling.

Miss Rosamond slept on sound, for all the wind blew so; and Miss Furnivall said never a word, nor looked round when the gusts shook the windows. All at once she started up to her full height, and put up one hand, as if to bid us listen.

'I hear voices!' said she, 'I hear terrible screams – I hear my father's voice!'

Just at that moment my darling wakened with a sudden start: 'My little girl is crying, oh, how she is crying!' and she tried to get up and go to her, but she got her feet entangled in the blanket, and I caught her up; for my flesh had begun to creep at these noises, which they heard while we could catch no sound. In a minute or two the noises came, gathered fast, and filled our ears; we, too, heard voices and screams, and no longer heard the winter's wind that raged abroad. Mrs Stark looked at me, and I at her, but we dared not speak. Suddenly Miss Furnivall went towards the door, out into the ante-room, through the west lobby, and opened the door into the great hall. Mrs Stark followed, and I durst not be left, though my heart almost stopped beating for fear. I wrapped my darling tight in my arms and went out with them. In the hall the screams were louder than ever; they sounded to come from the east wing – nearer and nearer – close on the other side of the locked-up doors – close behind them. Then I noticed that the great bronze chandelier seemed all alight, though the hall was dim, and that a fire was blazing in the vast hearth-place, though it gave no heat; and I shuddered up with terror, and folded my darling closer to me. But as I did so, the east door shook, and she, suddenly struggling to get free from me, cried, 'Hester, I must go! My little girl is there; I hear her; she is coming! Hester, I must go!'

I held her tight with all my strength; with a set will, I held her. If I had died my hands would have grasped her still, I was so resolved in my mind. Miss Furnivall stood listening, and paid no regard to my darling, who had got down to the ground and whom I, upon my knees now, was holding with both my arms clasped round her neck; she still striving and crying to get free.

All at once the east door gave way with a thundering crash, as if torn apart in a violent passion, and there came into that broad and mysterious light, the figure of a tall old man, with grey hair and gleaming eyes. He drove before him, with many a relentless gesture of abhorrence, a stern and beautiful woman, with a little child clinging to her dress.

'Oh, Hester! Hester!' cried Miss Rosamond. 'It's the lady! the lady below the holly trees; and my little girl is with her. Hester! Hester! let me go to her; they are drawing me to them. I feel them, I feel them. I must go!'

Again she was almost convulsed by her efforts to get away; but I held her tighter and tighter, till I feared I should do her a hurt; but rather that than let her go towards those terrible phantoms. They passed along towards the great hall door, where the winds howled and ravened for their prey; but before they reached that, the lady turned; and I could see that she defied the old man with a fierce and proud defiance; but then she quailed – and then she threw up her arms wildly and piteously to save her child – her little child – from a blow from his uplifted crutch.

And Miss Rosamond was torn as by a power stronger than mine, and writhed in my arms, and sobbed (for by this time the poor darling was growing faint).

'They want me to go with them on to the Fells – they are drawing me to them. Oh, my little girl! I would come, but cruel, wicked Hester holds me very tight.' But when she saw the uplifted crutch she swooned away, and I thanked God for it. Just at this moment – when the tall old man, his hair streaming as in the blast of a furnace, was going to strike the little shrinking child – Miss Furnivall, the old woman by my side cried out, 'Oh, Father! Father! spare the little innocent child!' But just then I saw – we all saw – another phantom shape itself, and grow clear out of the blue and misty light that filled the hall; we had not seen her till now, for it was another lady who stood by the old man, with a look of relentless hate and triumphant scorn. That figure was very beautiful to look upon, with a soft white hat drawn over the proud brows and a red and curling lip. It was dressed in an open robe of blue satin. I had seen that figure before. It was the likeness of Miss Furnival in her youth; and the terrible phantoms moved on, regardless of old Miss Furnivall's wild entreaty – and the uplifted crutch fell on the right shoulder of the little child, and the younger sister looked on, stony and deadly serene. But at that moment the dim lights and the fire that gave no heat went out of themselves, and Miss Furnivall lay at our feet stricken down by the palsy – death stricken.

Yes, she was carried to her bed that night never to rise again. She lay with her face to the wall muttering low but muttering always: 'Alas! alas! what is done in youth can never be undone in age! What is done in youth can never be undone in age!'